I know that what we write on the heart of a child cannot be erased and when a mother is at home to contribute to the **indelible marks that are written on a child's tender heart**, it is a rich heritage.

A child who has a mom at home during those special growing years is **indeed blessed.** Kathi Mills' book has captured this important precept...and I am sure it will be a **treasure for other moms** who are trying to piece together methods or formulas for successful mothering.

> Barbara Johnson
> Spatula Ministries
> La Habra, California

I love Kathi Mills. Many women have discovered the real problem with the rat race—that is that when the race is over you're still a rat.

If you need encouragement to do what **thousands of other women are doing, in returning to the home,** Kathi Mills' book *Mommy, Where Are You?* is the book for you.

> Kevin Leman, Ph.D.
> Author
> Tucson, Arizona

Amid a society so contorted, inverted, convoluted, and perverted as ours there is a **desperate need for a book like this**!

I'm not cynical about our society, nor am I prejudiced about the relative "career potential" of any given woman, but *someone* needs to shout, **"It's OK to be a Mom, a Wife, and a Keeper-of-the-home-fires!"** Kathi Mills is saying it! Loud and clear! And for that I thank her, and *urge* any and every thinking woman (and men too!) to tune in. **This is important to us all.** And *most* of all, to our kids and grandkids.

Jack W. Hayford, D.Litt.
Senior Pastor
The Church On The Way
Van Nuys, California

Mommy, Where Are You?

Kathi Mills

HARVEST HOUSE PUBLISHERS
Eugene, Oregon 97402

MOMMY, WHERE ARE YOU?

Copyright © 1992 by Kathi Mills
Published by Harvest House Publishers
Eugene, Oregon 97402

Library of Congress Cataloging-in-Publication Data

Mills, Kathi, 1948-
   Mommy, where are you? / Kathi Mills.
       p.   cm.
   ISBN 1-56507-057-7
       1. Mothers—United States.   2. Motherhood—United States—
Psychological aspects.   3. Motherhood—Religious aspects—Chris-
tianity   I. Title.
HQ759.M62   1992   92-12394
302.874'3—dc20   CIP

To my mom,
who was always there for me;
and to some other very special mommies—
Christy, Cathy, Shelly, and Terri,
the mommies to my grandchildren.
I love you all!

Contents

I Love My Mom Because...

Mother's Day, 1954. I had just turned six years old. My palms were sweaty, my bony knees were knocking, and my heart was pounding in my ears as I waited for my turn to stand up and announce to my entire kindergarten class, along with a sizable group of very proud mothers, why I loved my mom.

"I love my mom because she's soft when I sit on her lap," one little girl whispered shyly, as embarrassed giggles engulfed the other children.

"I love my mom because she bakes me cookies," declared the freckle-faced boy across the aisle.

"I love my mom because she doesn't make me take naps anymore," added the curly-haired girl in front of me.

And then it was my turn.

"I...I love my mom because..." I stopped, horrified. I knew I loved my mom and I knew there were a hundred reasons why I did, but for the life of me I couldn't think of any one of them.

I turned and looked at the group of mothers seated in the back of the classroom. They were all smiling at me encouragingly, but my mom's smile was the biggest of the bunch. And definitely the most beautiful. That's when I remembered.

"I love my mom because she takes care of me when I'm sick," I said, then added, "and that's a lot!"

As I sat back down, I didn't even mind the giggles sweeping across the room because I knew I had thought of just the right reason why I loved my mom. A frail, asthmatic child, I had already logged more sick time in my six short years than most people do in a lifetime. But no matter how sick I was or how long I had to stay in bed, I could always count on one thing: Mom would be right there by my side.

That was 1954. It was a lot more common—and a lot easier—for moms to be at their children's side then than it is today. I was part of the "Donna Reed/Ozzie and Harriet/

Father Knows Best" generation. We didn't have to watch "Happy Days" on TV because we were living them. (Besides, we only got one channel on our black-and-white TV, and the most exciting thing that was ever on was wrestling or the test pattern.) When we called out, "Mommy, where are you?" we would hear her answer, "I'm in the kitchen, Honey, making your lunch." But when our children or our children's children call out, "Mommy, where are you?" they are likely to hear a daycare worker inform them, "Mommy's at work. She'll pick you up at 5:30, just like she always does. Now go play with the other children."

Recently a number of books have appeared on the lasting effects of the physically absent or emotionally detached father, and rightly so. By original design, a father is to be the head of the home—an active head, involved with every aspect of his family's life. But if a father is the head, the mother is the heart. And without a heart, there can be no life.

While a working mother was an oddity when I was twirling my hula hoop around my nonexistent hips and waiting for the ice cream truck to turn the corner onto our street so I could buy a seven-cent popsicle, the full-time stay-at-home mother today is fast becoming an endangered species. And even though fewer mothers than fathers are absent from the home due to death or divorce, the number of single-parent homes headed by fathers is growing. It is also important to remember that fathers don't have the corner on being emotionally detached from their children. Sadly, there are quite a few families where the mother is home all day, and yet is so entirely absorbed in her own cares and needs that when the children cry out, "Mommy, where are you?" no one answers.

How did this happen? How did we change from being a nation that honored motherhood right up there with the flag and apple pie to a country that demands the right to send mothers to war, leaving their children to be raised by Dad or Grandma or whoever is available? Is this progress?

Have we women finally begun to achieve equality? Or have we bought into the biggest lie since the serpent told Eve that disobeying God and eating of the tree of the knowledge of good and evil wouldn't bring about her death?

Noted psychologist and author James Dobson has said that the "sexual revolution and feminism are the biggest jokes men have ever played on women." Author Connie Marshner questions whether it is just a coincidence that, right after the law was changed in 1974 to include a wife's income when a couple applied for a home loan, housing prices skyrocketed to the point that it is now nearly impossible for a family to buy a home unless both parents are working. The fact that in 1948 the average family of four paid approximately 3.4 percent of their income in taxes and now pays closer to 25 percent also needs to be taken into account when considering why so many mothers have now been "liberated" to join the work force.

"Mommy, where are you?" is a cry being echoed throughout more and more homes across our land. Is it a cry that needs to be resolved, or is it merely a sign of the times, something that will fade away and be forgotten as memories of Mommy get pressed between the pages of history like some antiquated dinosaur?

I believe that the mass exodus of mothers from home over the last two or three decades is more than simply a problem that needs to be resolved. I believe it is an emergency situation, one that must be addressed quickly and seriously before it is too late. We are living in a generation of dishonored and discontented women, a generation which has to a large degree turned the raising of their children over to strangers because they believe there is no other way to survive.

God, however, always makes a way where there seems to be no way. In *Mommy, Where Are You?* we will look not only at the problems of a mother-absent home and how our country has arrived at the place where women are pressured into doing double duty as both breadwinner and homemaker, but we will also examine some practical and biblical options for families struggling to keep up with the constantly rising cost of living.

"Mommy, where are you?" is not a cry that can be left unanswered. When our children and grandchildren are asked to stand up in class and tell why they love their mothers, they need to be able to say something besides "I love my mom because she has a neat briefcase" or "I love my mom because she's the best little corporate raider this side of the Mississippi." They need to be able to say things like "I love my mom because she's soft when I sit on her lap" and "I love my mom because she takes care of me when I'm sick." Most of all, they need to be able to say, "I love my mom because when I call her she says, 'Here I am!'"

The Mother-Heart of God

CHAPTER 1

Father. What a privilege to be a child of God and be able to address Him by such an intimate term! It hasn't always been so. The concept of God as Father was not thoroughly understood in Old Testament times. God was often viewed as a demanding Deity in whose hands one's destiny could be decided with a flick of His mighty finger. How blessed we are to be living in New Testament times, when the term "Father God" is the accepted form of address for those of us who have become part of His family through faith in Jesus Christ.

But God as Father is not what I wish to discuss in this opening chapter. I believe there is another side to God— His "mother" side—that we need to understand and become acquainted with if we are to understand our own roles as mothers. After all, having been made in God's image, it is only fitting that He should be our role model as we seek to raise our children in a way that is pleasing to Him.

In the twenty-third chapter of Matthew we see Jesus, just prior to His discourse on the end times and His prediction of the destruction of Jerusalem by Titus in 70 A.D., overlooking the city and crying out, "O Jerusalem, Jerusalem, the one who kills the prophets and stones those who are sent to her! How often I wanted to gather your children together, *as a hen gathers her chicks under her wings*, but you were not willing!" (verse 37, italics mine). What a beautiful picture of mother love! In this case it is that very mother love that burns in God's heart for His children—even and especially those who are rebellious and refuse to come to Him.

Any mother who has ever had a rebellious child can certainly relate to this. Without a doubt we love those compliant, cooperative children who cause us little grief and anxiety during their growing-up years. But oh, how our hearts yearn for those rebellious ones who insist on defying us every step of the way, constantly veering off the paths we have marked out for them and heading straight into inevitable danger. How we long to stop them, to save them from the heartache that awaits them! But they will not listen. They will not allow us to gather them under our wings and protect them.

They want nothing to do with the Secret Place—that place of divine refuge located "under His wings" (see Psalm 91:4). And so we continue to pray, believing that God is faithful and will bring our wayward ones home to the Secret Place before it is too late.

But where did we just say that Secret Place was? Under His wings. That's right. Next to God's heart—God's *bosom*. The place where mothers nurture and feed their young. The place where Jesus longed to gather His people "as a hen gathers her chicks under her wings."

As I mentioned earlier, if a father is the head of the home, the mother is the heart. And without a heart there can be no life. God is definitely our heavenly Father, but He also has a mother's heart—that place of refuge where we are nourished and protected. Because God so completely encompasses all that is both Father and Mother, and because He created us in His own image, He ordained that we be placed in families that would also encompass both a father and a mother nature. And He ordained the roles of those within the family to fulfill His purposes for creating and ordaining families.

But maybe I just stepped on some toes. In fact, I'm sure of it, because my own are hurting a bit. You see, there's a part of me that bristles at the thought of fulfilling an "ordained role," because I immediately feel that I have just been disqualified from doing a lot of other fun and fulfilling things *for the plain and simple fact that I happen to be a woman.* There's something in me that doesn't like this destiny, and that something is called *rebellion.*

I'll admit it—I was one of those rebellious kids who flopped my defiant toe across every line my parents ever drew. I wasn't about to stay within any boundaries that I hadn't decided on myself, and that was that. I spent more time on restriction than all the other kids on the block combined. The fact that I was sickly as a young child had no bearing on this problem whatsoever. I was headstrong and independent from the word "go."

One of my mother's favorite stories is about the time we were getting ready to go shopping. I was not quite two years old, and at that time the only child, since my brothers were both younger than I and hadn't yet arrived on the scene. My mother had dressed me first, then hurried into her room to get herself ready. Apparently I thought she took too long, because when she finished dressing and came out of her room, I was already gone.

Somehow I had figured out how to open the front door, and off I'd gone down the street, toddling toward the bus stop with my purse slung over my arm. Thankfully, we lived a long city block from the bus stop, and my mother was able to catch up with me before I left our quiet neighborhood street and stepped out onto the busy avenue to cross over to the bus bench. When she grabbed me and asked me just what I thought I was doing, I informed her I was going "choppin'." If she hadn't figured it out before then, she knew at that moment she had her hands full.

It was only the beginning. Trying to get me to pick up my toys became a daily war, one that usually left us both in tears—tears of frustration for her, tears of anger for me (although the spankings probably had something to do with it too).

The teen years were the worst, however. I simply did what I wanted to do, knowing I would be grounded accordingly, but not too concerned about it, since when I was grounded I simply waited until everyone else had gone to sleep and then went out the bedroom window.

And yet my mother kept on loving me. My father did too, of course, but he worked two jobs most of my growing-up years and wasn't around nearly as much as my mother. Which is how it was back in the "Happy Days," right? Dad went to work, Mom stayed home with the kids. And, to be perfectly honest, I grew up thinking that's how it would be when I got married, too.

But times had already changed. When I got married at the ripe old age of 18, with dreams of rose-covered cottages and cherubic little Gerber babies cooing at me from their playpen, I had no idea that in a matter of two years I would be separated from my husband, with two tiny babies to raise and absolutely no job training or experience. On top of that, I had been diagnosed with cancer and soon became too ill to continue caring for my children. And so they went to live with their father.

Why am I telling you all this? Because I want you to know early on that, although I was born and raised in the "Happy Days" era, I have certainly had a lot of days in my life that were less than happy. And in case you're thinking, "Well, sure, it's easy for *her* to tell me to stay home with my kids. What does she know? She's probably never had to struggle financially, never been a single mom...."

Guess again. But if I learned anything from those times, it's this: No matter how difficult life might get financially, there is *nothing* worth separating you from your children. True, God has restored my health and my children to me (not to mention the wonderful bonus of grandchildren), and I am now happily married to a supportive Christian man who is not only my best friend but my number one fan besides. But it hasn't always been that way. I know firsthand the price a mother pays—and the even greater price paid by her children—when a child calls out, "Mommy, where are you?" and no one is there to answer.

And so, now that you know my basic qualifications for writing this book, let's get back to our God-ordained roles as mothers. While much of our society currently views motherhood as some extracurricular activity to be squeezed in somewhere between career and personal pursuits, God has a different idea. In the Old Testament, the Hebrew word for mother means "the bond of the family." Hardly sounds like some incidental hobby to be tacked on to an already-overcrowded schedule, does it? As a matter of fact, using that definition, isn't it reasonable to assume that, without a mother, the family falls apart simply because there is nothing to hold it together? Suddenly motherhood takes on a whole new importance, doesn't it? Especially when you understand that, as families disintegrate, so does society.

Theodore "Teddy" Roosevelt understood this fact better than most when he declared, "If the mother does not do her duty, there will be either no next generation, or a next generation that is worse than none at all." Inherent in his statement is the implication that as mothers we have a definite duty. A role. A God-given assignment. And if we don't carry out that assignment, we will all suffer the consequences.

So now let's get down to brass tacks and discover just what that role or assignment is. And how better to discover that assignment than to check out the handbook on proper parenting written by our heavenly Father Himself—the Father who also has a mother's heart?

One of my favorite descriptions of motherhood is found in Psalm 113:9, "He grants the barren woman a home, like a joyful mother of children." Did you catch that adjective there? *Joyful.* God has ordained that motherhood be a joyful experience! And yet, those of us who have put in more than a few years in the profession know that at times motherhood is definitely less than joyful. Why?

I believe it's because we are not living within the boundaries God has ordained for motherhood, and therefore we are failing to fulfill our purpose as mothers. If God is indeed the One who created and established families, He is also the One who created and established the functions and purposes for families, including each individual member of those families. When we fail to follow the directions of our Creator, we will fail to function properly.

For instance, how many of you are like me and hate to read directions? I'll never forget when I first got my computer; I was so excited at the prospect of being able to write on the word processor. But when the salesman handed me three manuals full of directions for my computer and word processor, each marked "Read Me First," I knew I was in trouble. I am the kind of person that relates only to "user-friendly" directions, such as: "First, do this"; "second, do this"; "never, *ever* do this"; etc. And of course these user-friendly directions must be limited to no more than one page. So I called a friend who has the same type of computer and asked him to show me the bare essentials so I could use the word-processing part of my computer. Because I am intimidated by the direction manuals, I have never learned to avail myself of over 90 percent of my computer functions!

I am not a direction-follower by nature—and neither are you. Although God originally designed us with the intent that we would listen to and obey His divine instructions, Adam and Eve changed all that when they committed high treason in the Garden of Eden. God told them not to eat of the fruit of the tree of the knowledge of good and evil or they would die, but they chose to believe the lie of the serpent and disobeyed God's instructions. Ever since then, due to the fallen nature we inherited from those two non-direction-followers, we too tend to disbelieve God's instructions and try to do things our own way. Without exception, it never works.

True, when we were born again we inherited a new nature—God's nature—and this new nature desires to please God, which includes following His directions as laid out in His Word. But have you noticed that the old nature (which, although dead, seems intent on resurrection) continues to fight us every step of the way? It is only as we determine to read and obey God's directions daily that we begin to see the new nature manifest itself in our lives. It isn't easy. Most of the time the only way we can follow God's directions is to choose to obey in faith, even though the old "dead" nature is screaming at us to trust in our own understanding rather than God's. But Proverbs 3:5 is very clear about this issue: "Trust in the Lord with all your heart, and lean not on your own understanding; in all your ways acknowledge Him, and He shall direct your paths."

There's that word again: "direct." Sounds a lot like "directions," doesn't it? But if we are ever to become the joyful mothers we were designed to be, we are going to have to follow the Manufacturer's directions. So let's look again at God's Handbook on proper parenting to gain some more insight into motherhood.

One of the primary responsibilities of a mother is to teach the Word of God to her children. Proverbs 1:8 shows that this responsibility should be a joint effort between parents: "My son, hear the instruction of your father, and do not forsake the law of your mother." The father's part, however, is *instruction*, which is defined in the Hebrew and Chaldee dictionary of Strong's Concordance as: "chastisement; warning or instruction; also restraint: bond, chastening, chastisement, check, correction, discipline, doctrine, instruction, rebuke"; it is taken from the Hebrew root word meaning "bind, chasten, chastise, correct, instruct, punish, reform, reprove, sore, teach."

On the other hand, the mother's part, according to that Scripture, has to do with God's law, or His Word, the Bible. We know this because the Hebrew meaning for the word "law" in this Scripture is "Torah," referring to God's written word in existence at that time, particularly the Pentateuch or first five books of the Old Testament. It is obvious from these two definitions that, although it is both the mother's and father's responsibility to teach God's Word and His ways to their children, the father is to be more involved with disciplining, whereas the mother's primary responsibility is to teach her children from God's Word.

This is quite interesting when you realize that it is also the mother who is primarily responsible for feeding and nourishing her children physically, especially as nursing infants. It is then, as we mentioned earlier, that a mother holds her child close to her bosom, as the Father longs to hold us close in the Secret Place (see Psalm 91). It follows, then, that it is a mother's responsibility to feed her children spiritually as well as physically, and the only way to do that is to teach them God's Word.

When Jesus was tempted in the wilderness by Satan, He defeated him each time by quoting the Word of God. One of Satan's temptations appealed to Jesus' physical need for food, which was considerable after having fasted for 40 days. In Matthew 4:3,4, when Satan said to Him, "If You are the Son of God, command that these stones become bread," Jesus' answer was from Deuteronomy 8:3: "Man shall not live by bread alone, but by every word that proceeds from the mouth of God." This is a teaching that shows it is only our temporary, physical beings that are nourished and strengthened by the food we eat, whereas our eternal, spiritual beings are nourished and strengthened by feeding on the Word of God.

In 1 Peter 2:2 we clearly see this analogy of God nourishing His children through His Word as a mother nourishes her children at her bosom: "As newborn babes, desire the pure milk of the word, that you may grow thereby." First

Corinthians 3:2 takes the analogy a step further when the apostle Paul says, "I fed you with milk and not with solid food; for until now you were not able to receive it, and even now you are still not able." He is indicating here that Christians start out with the basics of the Word of God and then, as they grow and mature, move on to "meatier" issues. The same, of course, is true in the physical realm. But no one starts out on meat. All children, whether physical or spiritual babes, must be nourished in the bosom of their caretaker, whether it be their earthly mother or their heavenly Father.

Now I don't mean to imply for one minute that teaching our children the Word of God is our only function or responsibility in life. God has bestowed upon each of us various gifts and talents, which He expects us to use. "Mother" doesn't necessarily have to be our only title, but I believe the points we've discussed throughout this chapter give strong evidence that it should be our most important one, and one for which we should receive honor and respect. But even within the title of "Mother" it is obvious that we are called on to do more than teach the Word of God. There are countless physical and emotional needs that must be met daily when raising children. But it's important that we keep our temporal responsibilities in proper perspective, and we can only do that by concentrating on our eternal responsibilities, as this poem, which I wrote several years ago, so vividly emphasizes.

Remembering Mother

When all the children have grown and gone,
Which memories of Mother will linger on?
Will it be the times she dried their tears,
Held them close, and calmed their fears?

The way she always found the time
To read their favorite nursery rhyme
Over and over, time and again,
Until they knew it, beginning to end.

The sleepless nights with an ailing child,
Mother stayed there all the while,
Ministering love with healing hands,
Spinning tales of faraway lands.

What memories will follow them as they go?
All of these, and more, I know;
But most important, can they say,
"She loved God's Word and taught me to pray"?

God's primary purpose for us as mothers is to convey to our children the mother-heart of God, that nurturing love that draws us close to His bosom, safe in the Secret Place, where, as Psalm 91:10 promises us, "No evil shall befall you." If we can instill that kind of security in our children as we teach them of God's everlasting love for them, we will have successfully carried out our assignments as mothers. And without fail the day will come when our children will rise up and call us blessed (see Proverbs 31:28).

What other of life's rewards could ever begin to compare with that!

Good Mommies/ Bad Mommies

CHAPTER 2

"Moms in Touch." "Home by Choice." "Mothers at Home." Ever hear those names? If you haven't, you will—and soon. Groups of stay-at-home mothers are springing up everywhere, coming together to support each other, their families, and their choice of lifestyle. But does this mean that mothers who are not at home by choice are not in touch with their families? Are the working mothers the "Bad Mommies" and the stay-at-home mothers the "Good Mommies"?

That controversy has probably always been around to some degree or another, but it has been raging for the last two or three decades since the feminist movement gained momentum, resulting in a mass exodus of mothers from home and into the work force. Some of those mothers left home joyfully, believing that at last they had been freed from the drudgery of being "just a housewife." Others felt forced into the choice by economic demands, making the move with varying degrees of uncertainty—and lots and lots of guilt.

And that is the crux of the whole thing: Guilt. Legitimate or not, guilt haunts mommies in both camps, and it is a painful, ongoing problem. And this, of course, is why many of us choose to ignore or deny it: It's just too painful to deal with.

But deal with it we must, if we are ever to resolve the "Good Mommy/Bad Mommy" issue and make peace with our choice. And the only way to effectively deal with that guilt is to realize and understand the true facts in this issue of Working Moms versus Stay-at-Home Moms.

If we were to accept the image of motherhood portrayed by much of the media, we would believe that practically every woman in America between the ages of 18 and 65 is gleefully employed in a fulfilling, full-time job or career away from home. (Other than "Leave It to Beaver" reruns, when did you last see a TV sitcom with an intelligent, fulfilled, well-adjusted, stay-at-home mom? I rest my case.) We would also believe that the tiny minority of women who have elected to stay home and raise their children have done so because they are simply too lazy or uneducated or untalented to get a "real job." Hopefully, however, we have enough sense not to believe everything we read and/or hear from the media.

In actuality, according to the Department of Labor, Bureau of Labor Statistics, as of March 1990, 66.7 percent of mothers with children under the age of 18 were participating in the labor force; that figure drops to 58.2 percent for mothers with children under the age of six. And of that percentage, many were working only part-time, often during the hours their children were in school. A 1990 Monitor survey, one of the country's oldest annual surveys of social attitudes, found that, even among those women who were working outside the home, the desire to return home was increasing, while the love affair with jobs and careers was decreasing.

"We haven't talked about these numbers in public because they're so startling," says Susan Hayward, Senior Vice President of Yankelovich Clancy Shulman in Westport, Connecticut, in an April 1991 *American Demographics* article titled "New Women's Revolution" and written by Rebecca Piirto. "It's a tremendous change in one year. But I think it shows something big."

I believe this "something big" is a God-given desire in every mother's heart to rear and nurture her own children. We can try to ignore that desire, deny that desire, bury that desire. But it just won't go away. Hence the working mother's guilt.

"I miss my children terribly," says Marian, who drops her two preschoolers off at the daycare center at 7:30 every morning, picking them up again just before 6:00 P.M. "I tell myself it's a wonderful daycare, they're well cared for, we need the money from my job...but no matter how many reasons I come up with to justify being away from my children all day, the guilt is still there...and it's growing."

Guilt. Is it caused by a legitimate call from God for mothers to return home and care for their children? Or is it caused by an illegitimate call from society to be a "super-woman," able to leap from career woman to homemaker in a single bound, without missing a beat or sacrificing either role?

It's both. In Chapter 1, we looked at the mother-heart of God, and we saw that, because we have been created in the image of God, He is to be our role model for proper mothering. In God's plan for families, motherhood has a high priority. Even though He intends for it to be a joyful task, it is not a simple one, nor is it one that can be slotted in between the marketing and an aerobics class on Saturday morning. In this case the guilt is legitimate, and therefore must be dealt with in a way that will bring peace between our own mother-hearts and God's.

But what about the illegitimate guilt imposed on us by society to "do all," "be all," "have it all"? Is that possible, or are we beating our heads against the wall, striving to achieve the unachievable? Although some women may claim to be balancing it all successfully, more and more women are experiencing a growing frustration as they attempt to do so.

The *American Demographics* article "New Women's Revolution" states that previous Monitor surveys showed that two decades ago women were readily giving up their traditional homemaker roles in favor of pursuing careers. Five years ago, however, the survey showed that women were becoming dissatisfied with their hectic lives. The findings of the 1990 survey emphasize women's demands that their work lives change to accommodate their home lives. In fact, for the first time in 20 years the survey showed that less than 50 percent of women thought mothers should pursue a career outside the home. And 56 percent of working women polled said they would gladly quit work and stay home if they didn't absolutely need the money—up from 35 percent in 1987!

Yet the vast majority of media continues to bombard us with images of the successful career and family woman who jogs every morning, then zips home and feeds her family a nutritious breakfast before running out the door with her briefcase to conquer the world. When she arrives home that evening, her clothes are still neatly pressed and her hair in place as she cheerfully serves her husband and children a seven-course meal, then hurries upstairs to change into an evening dress so she and her husband can go out dancing.

I don't know about you, but I wouldn't last a week! And, according to Karen Scalf Linamen and Linda Holland, authors of *The Curious Waltz of the Working Woman*, I'm not alone.

Karen and Linda write, "Even though we all play a deceptive role in our own homes, we actually believe the ruse when we see it performed at someone else's. We actually walk away believing that other women are pulling it off: They're succeeding at being the perfect employee, perfect mother, perfect homemaker, perfect wife, perfect lover, ad nauseum. Which is just about as rational as thinking we all spend our weekends leaping tall buildings and running faster than bullets and stopping freight trains.

"The fact is, no one is making the grade.

"The *ultimate* fact is, the grade is simply unattainable."[1]

Again, guilt. But this guilt is illegitimate, placed upon us by a society that wants us to believe we really can do it all if we just: Get a little more organized, exercise more, eat right, read the right books, go to the right seminars. Bunk! The growing trend of frustrated and dissatisfied working mothers indicates that not only is it impossible to have it all, but women don't even want it! That built-in, God-given desire to stay home and nurture our children is rising up within mothers and crying out, "I'm sick of this guilt! I'm sick of being tired! I'm sick of being labeled a 'failure' because I can't do it all! I want to come home and raise my children, and find peace and respect in doing so!"

Even longtime feminist Betty Friedan, author of *The Feminine Mystique*, observed: "A woman thinks there is something wrong with her if she can't be a perfect corporate executive and at the same time a perfect wife and mother. Women in critical numbers are facing the agonies of this double burden."[2]

So why should we continue to allow these "double burdens" to be put upon us? God never intended it to be so. Jesus said, "Come to Me, all you who labor and are heavy laden, and I will give you rest. Take My yoke upon you and learn from Me, for I am gentle and lowly in heart, and you will find rest for your souls. For My yoke is easy and My burden is light" (Matthew 11:28-30). Again, we come back to the perfect parenting handbook, the Bible, authored by the One who knows everything there is to know about successful, fulfilling, and joyful motherhood. But if the words "successful, fulfilling, and joyful" don't describe the way you're feeling about your role as a mother—and "guilty" does—maybe it's time for you to throw off that illegitimate guilt put on you by society, resolve the legitimate guilt you're experiencing as a result of God's call to your mother-heart, and begin to experience the joyful motherhood God has ordained for you.

All right, I know—that's easier said than done. And I would be less than fair not to mention that there are some very valid reasons for women to work. Most single mothers, and even some married mothers, seemingly have no choice—or do they? We'll examine that in more detail in later chapters. But for now, if you are a working mother either by choice or by necessity, let's be honest here and face the fact that society has, in one way or another, influenced your decision to do double-duty at home and in the work force—and, along with that decision, has heaped a degree of guilt on you for not doing both jobs just a little bit better.

But you know what? Working moms aren't the only ones wrestling with guilt. Stay-at-home moms aren't exactly free of this problem either. True, their guilt may be somewhat different from that of working mothers, but it's still guilt, no matter how you look at it.

Many stay-at-home moms have chosen their situations in answer to that built-in desire to be with and nurture their children and therefore they probably aren't dealing with the type of guilt that stems from ignoring God's call on their lives to motherhood. However, society really does a number on these women.

First of all, they have been stereotyped by the media for the plain and simple reason that they have no current role models. As I said earlier, how often do you turn on the TV or go to the movies or read a book where the heroine is a full-time homemaker? Even school textbooks portray mothers as full-time career women; if you want to read a story about a stay-at-home mom, you've got to dig up an old copy of a "Dick and Jane" primer. And so our children grow up brainwashed into thinking that any intelligent, energetic, vital, interesting woman would naturally opt for a career over staying home and wiping runny noses all day.

But is that all there is to full-time mothering? Does a woman who chooses a homemaking career spend her days checking the kitchen floor for yellow wax buildup and refereeing sibling squabbles? Does her brain turn to mush as she limits her conversations to monosyllabic dialogues all day? Is she doomed to live her life vicariously through soap operas and romance novels? Or is it possible—just possible—that the stay-at-home mom is really the liberated woman after all?

"I love it," Laurie exclaimed when asked how she coped with full-time homemaking. "It's the best of all possible worlds. Really! I used to work—I was an escrow analyst at a large bank and was in line for a big promotion. Then Andy was born. Suddenly escrow figures—even increased salary figures—seemed quite dull and unimportant compared to watching my child grow up. I had planned to go back to work as soon as he was six weeks old, but by then I was so in love with him that there wasn't enough money in the world to convince me to leave him in someone else's care so I could go back to pursuing my career. My husband and I talked it over and we knew it would mean some difficult financial adjustments, but it's been worth it. What we gave up monetarily doesn't even begin to compare with what we've gained as a family.

"Do I miss my career, the interaction with other adults, the feeling of success and accomplishment that comes with job advancement? Oh, occasionally I get a twinge of regret. But then Andy comes and wraps his chubby arms around my neck and I know I've made the right choice.

"The only real problem is dealing with people who don't understand or agree with my decision. They keep insisting that I'm missing out on something, that I'm wasting all my training and experience. I just can't seem to convince them that raising Andy is so much more challenging and rewarding than any other career could ever be!"

Laurie is not alone. Countless stay-at-home moms find themselves unacceptable to a society that tries to heap guilt on them for "copping out," for not "going for the gold." But as these mothers begin to discover one another through groups like "Mothers at Home" and "Home by Choice," they will learn to stand tall and demand the respect due them for the vital job they are doing: raising our country's next generation.

But these stay-at-home moms need to understand that it's more than society's guilt they're up against. Government is making it increasingly difficult for mothers to stay at home with their children, pushing instead for "social parenting," a concept that is already in full swing in Sweden—and tragically so.

Connie Marshner, author of *Can Motherhood Survive?* explained in a Focus on the Family radio interview with James Dobson that the combination of socialism and feminism has been deadly in Sweden. That country now has laws requiring every nonhandicapped adult to be financially responsible for himself or herself. In other words, if a mother wants to stay home with her children, she can't do it. It is illegal for her husband to support her; she must go out and support herself, turning the care of her children over to the state.

Mrs. Marshner went on to give an example of a woman whose husband worked for the Swedish government. She wanted to stay home with their two children, so her husband asked for an annual raise of about $5000. He was turned down. Instead, she was forced to go to work, placing her children in a government-run daycare, which cost taxpayers approximately $32,000 per year—$27,000 more than if her husband had been granted the raise so she could stay home with their children!

Japan, on the other hand, has a very different attitude toward parenting. Only about 20 percent of the women in Japan are in the work force. Many of them quit their jobs when they marry; if not, they almost certainly quit upon the birth of their first child. And, although there is a nursery school system in Japan, the children attend only a few hours each day, while mothers are required to help the teachers and to be involved in every aspect of their children's education. Isn't it interesting that, at this point in time, Japan is our only really significant industrial rival?

And yet our country also once honored motherhood. As I said earlier, mothers who worked away from home were almost unheard-of when I was growing up, except possibly in single-parent families. And stay-at-home moms never felt the need to apologize for the fact that they greeted their children at the front door when they came home from school, or ran outside to kiss "boo-boos" when they heard an anguished cry coming from the backyard. Schools weren't at a loss to find room mothers to help out in their children's classrooms, and when they held a PTA meeting, people actually showed up!

Now, with families paying close to 25 percent of their income in taxes, nonemployed spouses limited to putting $250 annually into an IRA, and prices of homes so high that it is almost impossible even to qualify for a loan on one salary, our country is quickly moving to a place where social parenting could become the only viable option.

And just what is social parenting? It is the belief that someone other than the parents—preferably the government—can best raise children. A chilling thought for those of us who don't happen to agree! But don't think it can't happen. The ever-growing number of government-funded and private daycare centers proves that many of us are all too willing to abandon the care of our children to strangers while we go out in pursuit of the American dream—a dream that could all too quickly turn into a nightmare as our children reject our ideals and adopt those of their new "caretakers." We are already on the road to social parenting, speeding along in the fast lane, oblivious to the dead end ahead. If we continue to ignore the warning signs, we will have only ourselves to blame.

So what has all this got to do with "Good Mommies/Bad Mommies"? A lot! While we've been dividing up into camps, taking potshots at each other in a vain attempt to prove that we are the good mommies, the real enemy has been sneaking into both camps virtually undetected, using the smoke-screen of illegitimate guilt to hide its true objective—social parenting. All along we've been duped into thinking that the other camp is our enemy, when in reality our enemy would appear to be a social system that would press us into a mold we were never intended to fit!

And yet, I believe our true enemy is something even more sinister than a destructive social system. Our enemy is one and the same adversary that Adam and Eve faced in the Garden of Eden—Satan himself. Because God has designed the family unit with the intent of godly parents raising a generation of godly offspring, Satan has determined to destroy the family. What better way to do it than to devise a system that would remove children from the influence and protection of their parents?

It's time we mommies—good, bad, or somewhere in between—band together to fight for the common goal of what is best for our children. Whether you are a mother working away from home or a stay-at-home mom, if you agree that we are the ones who can best rear our own children, then our cause is a united one. Already many of the stay-at-home moms' groups, like those mentioned earlier in this chapter, are fighting for legislation that will ease financial pressures on families and help those mothers out there in the work force who desperately want to come home. Chapters of these groups are being organized throughout the country; getting involved in one locally will send a message of support and encouragement to the many other mothers fighting for the right to stay home and raise their children, as well as a warning to the social and governmental agencies—not to mention the demonic forces—that would usurp that right from us.

Moms, let's deal with our guilt by declaring a truce with

one another, recognizing the real enemy, and moving on to more productive ways of raising our children—ways that will be beneficial to them, fulfilling and joyful for us, and pleasing to our Father God, who also has a mother-heart.

I
Want
My Mommy!

CHAPTER 3

I'll never forget the first time I met James. A light-skinned African-American of about 17 or 18, his piercing brown eyes unnerved me. Even though I had ministered to inmates convicted of much more serious crimes than his, I was suddenly glad for the guards positioned strategically around the prison's visiting area.

Over the past few years since I have become involved in prison ministry, I've had the opportunity to visit several maximum-security prisons, even spending a day on death row at San Quentin. But none of them have affected me more deeply than the California Youth Authority facility in Camarillo, California. The inmate population at that facility consists of about 700 to 800 males and females between the ages of 13 and 25. Many of them are there for repeated drug offenses, some for gang-related activities, some even for murder. James' offense was minor compared to some of his fellow inmates, but his pain was not.

"You have any kids?" he asked me. I raised my eyebrows in surprise. Few of these young inmates were aggressive enough to initiate conversations with volunteers until they had seen them on the grounds several times, but this was the first time James and I had crossed paths.

"Yes," I replied. "But only one is still at home. The others are grown and married."

"You ever live in Mississippi?"

I shook my head. "No, I've never even been there."

He cocked his head to one side and his eyes narrowed. "You sure?" he demanded.

"I'm sure," I answered, wondering where all these questions were leading.

His shoulders seemed to sag and the intensity in his dark eyes faded to disappointment. "Oh," was all he said.

Sensing the need to pursue the conversation, I asked, "Is that where you're from—Mississippi?"

He hesitated, as if deciding whether or not to trust me. "Yes," he answered, almost in a whisper. "Originally. At least, that's what they tell me—that I was born there, I mean."

"I see," I said. "So your family moved away from there soon after you were born?"

At the mention of his family, his eyes blazed. "Which family?" he asked. "My real family or the one that lied to me all these years?"

This time it was my turn to hesitate. "I'm...not sure what you mean," I said.

James was fired up now and I could tell he wanted to talk. "I never saw my real dad," he said. "My mom, either. She gave me away when I was born. Then these other people adopted me and I grew up thinking they were my real parents. The only way I found out the truth was at a family reunion a couple years ago. I guess I came in when I wasn't supposed to and heard my mom talking to my aunt about my real mom. They were real upset when they saw me, but I made them tell me the whole story."

He paused for a moment, so I asked him, "Would you like to tell me about it?"

He studied me again. "You sure you never been in Mississippi?"

"Never."

He shrugged and dropped his eyes. "It's just that...

you're the right age and all...I mean, you know...you could be my...mom."

I caught my breath. So that was it! This angry, hurting young man was so in need of his mother that he would actually risk approaching a strange woman to see if maybe, just maybe, she might be his mom! I can't remember when I've had to fight so hard to hold back my tears.

James and I spent the next year getting to know each other. The more I learned of his life, the more my heart ached for him. He told me how he had run away soon after discovering the truth about his birth; it wasn't long before he was in trouble with the law. He also told me that he had since learned that, although his natural father and both of his adoptive parents were black, his mother was white. He wondered if that was the reason she had given him up. He wondered if she had been young and poor and unable to care for him; if she had really wanted him but just didn't know how to raise him; if he would ever find her and, if he did, if she would accept or reject him. Never once did he mention a desire to locate his natural father, but his longing for his mother had become an obsession.

Slightly over a year after I met James, he was paroled. Just before he left the prison, I asked him if he was going to go back home and try to work things out with his adoptive parents. He said no. Even though he knew it would violate the conditions of his parole, he planned to take as much time as necessary in crisscrossing the country, looking for his natural mother. I haven't heard from him since.

Although James' situation is a tragic one and different from that of most children, he is definitely not the only one crying out, "I want my mommy!" It is a cry that every daycare worker hears countless times throughout the long day. It can also be a silent cry, particularly when it is on the lips of a tiny, unborn baby, about to be sacrificed by the very one to whom that child is crying out for love and protection.

The spirit of abortion is prevalent in our land today, screaming for a woman's right to choose, drowning out the heartrending cries of our children who are calling out, "I want my mommy!" Jesus said, "Whoever receives one little child like this in My name receives Me. But whoever causes one of these little ones who believe in Me to sin, it would be better for him if a millstone were hung around his neck and he were drowned in the depth of the sea" (Matthew 18:5,6).

Now don't get me wrong. I'm not trying to equate leaving your child in a daycare center with having an abortion. But I am saying this: We have come to a place in our society where children are often viewed as a liability rather than an asset; a place where convenience takes precedence over responsibility and relationship; a place where "throwaway kids" are fast becoming a reality.

And this is the kind of environment in which we expect our children to grow up to be healthy, responsible adults. Daily they are exposed to drugs, gangs, violence, pornography, and every conceivable type of ungodly influence. Although as parents our value system may be diametrically opposed to all these destructive forces, if we abdicate our parental responsibility and accept the alternative of social parenting, how can we possibly expect our children to grow up untouched and unscathed by the darkness around them?

In *God's Lost Children*, Sister Mary Rose McGeady quotes these statistics:

- Every eight seconds of every school day, a child drops out of school;
- Every 26 seconds a child runs away from home;
- Every 67 seconds a teenager has a baby;
- Every seven minutes a child is arrested for drug abuse;
- Every 36 minutes a child is killed or injured by a gun;

- Every day 135,000 American children carry their guns with them to school.[1]

And the statistics become more and more grim all the time. According to the Department of Justice, Federal Bureau of Investigation, *Uniform Crime Reports for the United States, 1990,* there were a total of 1,355,638 males under the age of 18 arrested in the United States in 1990, up from 1,260,123 in 1989; females under the age of 18 arrested in 1990 were 398,904, up from 351,451 in 1989. These arrests were for various crimes, ranging from runaways and curfew violations to murder and aggravated assault.

These are our children we're talking about here—the next generation of Americans—children whose childhoods have been stolen from them and replaced with crime and violence and hopelessness. And yes, a large number of these children who get into trouble are from homes where no father is present, so I don't want to minimize for a moment the importance of a father in a child's life. But whether a child has a father or not, there is a need for nurturing within that child that can only be met by Mom.

I remember when I was doing some research for a writing project on homosexuality and AIDS. I visited a lot of hospital rooms and sat beside the beds of a lot of dying patients, but never once did I see a father present to comfort and console his son. Some died completely alone. But many had at least one faithful visitor right up to the end—Mom.

It's no different in prison. Although many inmates have no visitors at all, those who do will tell you the same thing time and again—it's Mom. When everyone else gives up on them, Mom's still there, loving them, encouraging them, praying for them.

And this is as it should be; God has designed it so. And yet as mothers we have allowed ourselves to get caught up in the "me" generation, believing that if we don't toot our own horns, nobody else will. But who's going to toot our children's horns? Are we going to abandon them to do it for themselves? If so, we can hardly blame them when they get caught up in the destructiveness of a generation awash in a chemical daze, listening to suicidal lyrics of groups who glorify Satan's trademarks of killing, stealing, and destroying. Is it any wonder that the suicide rate of teens is increasing to terrifying proportions?

When I got the call about Linda's third suicide attempt in a month, I wasn't surprised. Distressed, yes, but not surprised. Linda was not quite 18, serving the third year of a ten-year sentence for murder.

Linda was not your typical youth authority inmate. An only child, raised in an affluent home where both of her parents had successful careers, Linda had spent most of her growing-up years with a babysitter or "nanny." But when she hit her freshman year in high school, her parents decided to send her away to boarding school. Although they told her they were doing it so she could get a better education, she was sure it was because they just didn't want her around anymore. She ran away.

Once out on the streets, Linda had no idea what to do to make a living. Attractive and physically mature for her age, she received a lot of propositions from men and could easily have supported herself as a prostitute, as so many young teens do. But Linda just couldn't bring herself to do it. Instead, she got involved in a drug delivery scheme. She was the middle person, delivering drugs from the dealer to the user. When a delivery of heroine turned out to be lethal, killing three of its users, Linda was the one arrested for their murders. Because of her age and the fact that she had no previous record, she received a relatively light term of ten years.

But to Linda, ten years was not a light term—it was forever. She was terrified of going to prison, sure she would never make it out alive. She spent as much time as possible in her cell, coming out only when absolutely necessary.

Because hers was a single-bunk dorm, she had no room-mate to befriend her. It wasn't long before the other in-mates decided she was a snob and avoided her entirely. The fear and isolation drove Linda to the point where suicide seemed the only option.

Thankfully, Linda is still alive today, and beginning to make some progress. The turnaround came after that third suicide attempt when her mother, who had refused even to attend Linda's trial, agreed to visit her daughter in prison. Slowly the walls between them are coming down, and love and trust are beginning to bridge the gap. Recently, at Linda's mother's urging, Linda's father agreed to come along on one of the visits. I can only pray that, by the time Linda's sentence is completed, this shattered family will have found its way to wholeness.

But must we wait until tragedy strikes to begin to spend time with our children? Not every family has the oppor-tunity for restoration, as I learned so vividly from Anita.

Anita was a middle-aged woman whose husband had died when her two children were still in diapers. With the help of babysitters, she had raised them alone, working full-time throughout their growing-up years. Julie had never given her any trouble. A sweet, compliant child, she and Anita had shared a special closeness that had, in Anita's words, "more than made up for our not having a husband or father."

But Jonathan was different. Less than a year older than Julie, he was headstrong and defiant, stubborn and unco-operative. He resented the closeness his mother and sister shared; he resented even more that his father had died and left him to grow up with two females who, he decided early on, really didn't like him very much. He had his first homo-sexual encounter when he was 13. By the time he was 17 he had had lovers too numerous to count. Soon after this he ran away and lived on the streets, making a profitable living as a prostitute. Somehow he thought AIDS would never happen to him.

By the time I met Jonathan, he was dying. He spent his last days on a respirator, his senses dulled by massive injections of morphine. His mother was finally located, and she rushed to his bedside only two days before he slipped away. Crying while she stroked his pale, thin hand, she told him of her love for him. I prayed that somehow he could hear her.

"If only I'd told him sooner," she cried. "If only his father hadn't died. If only I'd spent more time with him. If only..."

Anita will have to learn to receive God's forgiveness, as well as her own, if ever she is to be free of her "if onlys...." Even sadder than a mother's "if onlys," however, are a child's.

My first thought upon meeting David was, "This child does not belong in prison." A slightly built Hispanic youth, his soft-spoken, gentle mannerisms seemed in stark contrast with his attempted murder conviction. And yet, he assured me, he had at one time been a violent, drug-abusing gang member. After six months at the youth authority, during a prison ministry crusade, he had accepted Jesus Christ as his Savior. His favorite Bible verse was 2 Corinthians 5:17: "Therefore, if anyone is in Christ, he is a new creation; old things have passed away; behold, all things have become new." David was indeed a walking testimony to the truth of that Scripture.

But David still had some "if onlys" that plagued him almost daily. "If only I had known the Lord before my mom died," he lamented. "Maybe I could have told her about Him and she could have been delivered from drugs like I was. But now it's too late for her. She died of an overdose just before I was arrested."

David's mother had been a drug addict. It was the only role model David had ever known. Sadly, he followed in her footsteps. It landed him in prison. True, good came out of it in that he became a Christian and now plans to go to Bible college when he is paroled, but as he said, "It's too late for my mom."

I know the examples I have given are extreme cases, but in each instance a child is crying out, "I want my mommy!" It is a haunting cry, one that should never go unanswered, and yet it does—daily. From the abortion clinics to daycare centers to AIDS-care hospitals to youth prisons, "I want my mommy!" is the heartcry of countless American children. None of us can answer all their cries, but surely we can answer a few of them—especially the cries of those children living within our own homes.

Isn't it worth a try? Isn't it worth doing whatever is necessary so that when our own children call out, "I want my mommy," we can be there to answer that cry? Aren't a few sacrifices now better than risking a life of "if onlys" later?

True, staying at home with our children doesn't guarantee that they will never get into trouble. But with all they're up against every day, they need all the help they can get. Coming home to a mom who cares has got to be a lot more affirming than coming home to an empty house and an afternoon spent in front of the TV watching cartoons and rock videos.

Considering all the negative influences bombarding our children these days, perhaps it would be wise to heed the words of one high school teacher who said, "I don't believe kids turn to their peers because they are close to them or even because they like them that much. Sometimes they go to their peers by default. Nobody's home."[2]

Nobody's home. Is that what our children discover when they come home wanting mommy? If so, maybe it's time to reevaluate our priorities and give our children what they really need—their mommies.

The mother-heart of God would have us do no less.

What About Mr. Mom?

CHAPTER 4

Over the years, Hollywood has had a lot of fun portraying bumbling, inept fathers trying to care for and raise their children. We've all giggled at the scene of the harried dad holding a screaming baby with a toddler hanging on his leg while the washing machine spurts suds onto the laundry room floor and pots and pans are boiling over on the stove. But why is it so funny? Why do we mothers laugh the loudest at these hilarious characters affectionately dubbed "Mr. Mom"?

Because we're married to them, that's why. Oh, I know there are a few exceptions, but overall, Mr. Mom is not such a farfetched character. I mean, think about it. Even the most modern father—you know, the one who rushes home from work to "bond" with his offspring—gladly hands him back to Mom when Junior starts crying.

"Here, you take him," says Dad. "He wants something and I don't know what it is."

As if you do, right? And yet Dad assumes that, if anyone can figure out what Junior wants, it must be Mom. What do you do with logic like that? Well, unless you like to listen to your child cry indefinitely, you find out what he wants and take care of the problem ASAP.

My point is, there seems to be some sort of unwritten law that proclaims mothers to be the ultimate source of wisdom when it comes to discovering and meeting their children's needs. No matter how hard Mom tries to "share" housework and childcare with her husband, she still ends up with the lion's share of the work.

Now if Mom is able to stay home all day to take care of this work, maybe this is fine. But what about if both Mom and Dad are putting in a full day at the office, only to come home to crying, hungry kids who need help with their homework and rides to dancing lessons and soccer practice? And this doesn't even begin to take into account the need to make dinner, wash dishes, do the laundry, mop the sticky kitchen floors, and put clean sheets on the beds.

I have talked to countless couples where both Mom and Dad work away from home and who claim to share the housework and child-rearing duties. But upon closer examination, Dad's share usually amounts to going out into the backyard after work to play catch with the kids while Mom makes dinner. After dinner, Dad clears the table and then goes and plops in his favorite chair to watch the evening news. Mom, on the other hand, has to finish the dishes, supervise homework and baths, toss in a load of laundry, and pack lunches for the next day.

Weekends aren't any better. Dad may offer to do the grocery shopping, but guess who has to stop and make up the list? Meanwhile, on her two days "off," Mom tries to clean the entire house and catch up on the laundry and ironing; somewhere in between all that, she hopes to squeeze in some "quality" time with the kids.

Even with the best of intentions, Mr. Mom just doesn't cut it. And sooner or later Mrs. Mom is going to feel more than a little resentful—not to mention cranky and exhausted. Is it worth it?

Danielle doesn't think so. "I worked full-time all the years my kids were growing up," she recalls. "I really didn't want to, but my husband insisted. He said we just couldn't make it on his salary, and it wasn't fair for him to have to pull all the weight financially. So I stuck my kids with sitters and went out and found a job. My kids suffered because I was never there for them. My husband suffered because I never had any time or energy left over to do anything fun or enjoyable. And I suffered physically and emotionally. I felt torn, wanting to help financially but wanting also to be home with my children. I have to admit, over the years I became resentful—not so much of my husband's insistence that I work, but of the situation in general. Now that my kids are almost grown and gone, I feel cheated. I know I missed something very special that I can never get back. And I'm tired—just plain tired. I feel like an old woman before my time."

Admittedly, Danielle's husband was little or no help with the house or the kids, so Danielle pulled double-duty for years. But how much different is it for those women whose husbands are willing to help out at home?

"Not much," admits Brenda, smiling wryly. "Oh, don't get me wrong. Chuck tries to help. After work, we supposedly split the household and childcare duties. But somehow his duties always end up taking him about 15 minutes, while mine take more like three hours." Her smile widened. "Besides, even when he does try to help, I usually end up having to go back and 'fix' things, if you know what I mean."

We know what she means, right? We've all seen Mr. Mom in action, if not at home, then at least at the movies. But what about when Mr. Mom—or Mrs. Mom—has no choice but to pull double-duty?

I'm talking about single parents—and their numbers are legion! The Department of Commerce, Bureau of the Census, reports that in 1990 the number of families in the United States headed by mothers with children under 18 and with no father present in the home was 11,378,000. And don't think that Mr. Mom doesn't exist, because he does, and his numbers are growing right along with the number of single-parent homes headed by women.

According to figures in the June 16, 1991, edition of the *Los Angeles Times*, the number of single-parent homes headed by men in Ventura County, California, jumped 74 percent from 1980 to 1990, making an increase from 2957 households to 5159. The increase in single-parent homes headed by mothers during that same period in the county was only 19 percent.

What does that tell us? Gina Giglio, a counselor with Ventura Family Center, Inc., says, "It is a sad testament to the breakdown of the family in America." It is also a sad testament to the decline of motherhood.

Years ago, just about the only father you found raising his children was the one whose wife had died. Now men are often left to raise their children because their wives have decided there is something else they would rather do than be mothers.

One can only wonder how this grieves the mother-heart of God. As our society moves toward a place where the unisex trend is fast becoming a reality, our children are the ones being sacrificed on the altar of "progress." And, although some single parents are raising their children alone by choice, many are being forced to do so by default. Both men and women are leaving their mates and children behind to fend for themselves as best they can. Sometimes that "best" can be pretty rough.

Statistics show that after a divorce a single mother's income is cut *at least* in half. In addition, according to the U.S. Department of Labor, Bureau of Labor Statistics, in 1990 the average weekly earnings of the full-time working woman was only 71.8 percent of a full-time working man. Those facts, combined with the lamentable truth that a vast number of absent fathers pay little or no child support, show why single-parent homes headed by women are often struggling financially.

However, the Mr. Mom families aren't doing much better. Although the single-parent father may well be making more money with which to support his family than the single-parent mother, the financial worth of a stay-at-home mom must be taken into account here.

Well-known financial analyst Sylvia Porter claims that the approximately 25 million full-time homemakers in this country contribute billions to our economy annually. Most people are not aware of this because their labor is not counted in the gross national product.[1]

Sadly, states Porter, the full-time mother and home-maker is considered "economically nonexistent." Yet when Porter calculated how much money the stay-at-home mom actually adds to her family's economic standards, Porter concluded that few families—and this includes the Mr. Mom families—could afford to hire someone to replace that stay-at-home mom. Her findings showed that the annual salary of someone who performed all the duties of a full-time homemaker and mom would average between $23,580 and $28,735. I wonder how many mothers with full-time employment away from home make anywhere near that much.

In fact, I can't help but wonder how many mothers employed outside the home have really sat down and fig-ured out just how much money they are making. If, for instance, you have a full-time clerical position earning $350 per week (and many clerical positions pay much less), depending on your payroll deductions, you might take home about $250 of that. If you have two children in full-time daycare, you've just spent an average of $75 (and that's a conservative figure). Now we're down to $175. Assuming you drive an economical car and live only 10 to 15 miles from your workplace, the cost of gas could average around $10 weekly, leaving you with $165 for the week. Should there be additional upkeep costs on the car due to the extra miles driven to and from work, your weekly profit drops even more.

Now when you consider that you've got to dress a bit nicer to go to work in an office than you would if you were staying home all day, we'll take out a very conservative clothing allowance of $25 per week. If you go out for lunch even two or three days each week (which many working people do), you've just spent another $15. And don't forget how tempting it is to pick up fast food on the way home to avoid cooking dinner—another $15 to $20 for a family of three or four. If you do that even twice a week, you have just lowered your actual weekly profit to about $85.

I ask you—do you really love your job that much that you're willing to leave your children at a daycare for nine or ten hours each day while you head to the office so you can bring in an additional $85 per week? It seems to me a pitiful trade-off for the sacrifices involved.

On the other hand, what's the alternative? As a single parent, there often seems to be none. In a later chapter, however, we will discuss some very real and practical ideas that just might help you find that alternative, if you're truly in the market for one. In the meantime, suffice it to say that I sincerely empathize with the single parent's plight—I've been there, remember? But as a divorced mother, I quickly learned that the Scripture "For your Maker is your husband" (Isaiah 54:5), commonly known as "the widow's verse," also applies to divorced women—and I claimed it often!

It was never easy, and yet, probably because of my experience of being separated from my children for a time, the financial struggle seemed unimportant in comparison. Sure, I had to work for awhile, but I was able to find a job at a daycare where my youngest was with me during the day. It didn't pay much salary-wise, but it was worth it to me to be with my son. Besides, they didn't charge me anything for having him there with me, so that in itself was a big financial help.

By the time my youngest was in school all day, I had found a much-better-paying job working for a Christian couple's construction company. It was only a few blocks from home and school, which eased my mind a lot. A few times, when I had a sick child who couldn't go to school, they either let me take my work home or bring my child to work with me, allowing him to nap or watch TV in the employees' lounge. I will forever be indebted to them for their understanding and compassionate attitude!

But as I said, it wasn't easy. There were a lot of financial struggles and sacrifices, not to mention times when I felt a complete failure as a mom. I was totally vindicated, however, by a recent comment from one of my sons.

"You know, Mom," he mused, "looking back, I'd say my best memories are from when we lived in that little apartment over on Shenandoah Street. Remember how we used to eat popcorn and watch TV on Saturday nights? That was great!"

Great? The only reason we ate popcorn and watched TV (on a very tiny black-and-white set, by the way) was because we couldn't afford to do anything else. But he thought it was great! I could have kissed him. (Actually, I did.)

So I hope that encourages you if you're in that position at the moment. What you may now think of as trials and struggles might just become your children's best memories. Isn't God good?

You bet He is! And, as I said, whether you're widowed, divorced, or never married, that Scripture in Isaiah 54 applies to you. In fact, if you're a single-parent father, it applies to you too. If you'll let Him, He will be a Husband to you. He will love you and care for you and provide for you in ways you've never imagined. But don't just take my word for it. Listen to some of the other Mr. and Mrs. Moms I've talked to.

"When John first left us, I thought I was losing my mind," Shirley recalls. "Here I was with three little kids, no job, no money. It was terrible! I had never felt so alone, so betrayed—so utterly helpless! John and I had been married right out of high school and I'd never held down a job in my life. All I knew how to do was take care of kids, which was something I dearly loved, but I sure never thought I could make a living off of it.

"However, when I started pounding the pavement, looking for work and finding nothing that paid enough even to survive on, I started getting desperate. I can't tell you the times I cried myself to sleep, begging God to show me what to do to support my children. And then, one night as I was praying and reading the Bible, I came across Isaiah 54:5, and I said out loud, 'Well, God, if you're my Husband, then I guess I don't have anything to worry about. So I'm just going to go to sleep now and trust You for a solution to all this.'

"By the next morning I had my answer. I would open a daycare center in my home! After all, it's what I knew and loved. Why not make some money off it and still get to stay home with my kids? So I started phoning around to see what was required to open my home for daycare. It took awhile to get licensed, but it sure didn't take any time at all until my quota of kids was full—and I had a waiting list a mile long!

"My kids are almost raised now, and I've never had to be away from home to support them. I'm not sure how much longer I'll continue to operate the daycare from my home— I suppose as long as I'm physically able. But I'm not worried. When it comes time for me to close the daycare, my faithful Husband will provide for me in some other way. I can hardly wait to see what it is!"

Margaret's solution was born out of the same desperation. Widowed at 28, with a six-month-old baby to raise, she considered going back to her job as a florist, possibly even using some of her husband's insurance money to open her own shop. But she just couldn't bear the idea of leaving her tiny daughter.

The answer came to her one day during a young mothers' weekly Bible study. As Margaret sat cuddling her baby, listening to one of the other mothers reading from Isaiah 54, verse 5 seemed to jump out at her. "My Husband," thought Margaret. "God is my Husband! Well, if that's the case, He will also take care of me and my child. I'm not sure how, but—"

"Margaret," said the woman next to her, "it's your turn to read."

Margaret looked startled. "Excuse me?" she asked.

"It's your turn to read," repeated the woman, smiling gently. "It seems your mind was somewhere else."

Margaret nodded, then shared with the other women what she had been thinking, and how she had been so concerned about finding a way to supplement her late husband's insurance money while still staying home to raise her daughter.

"Well, let's pray," suggested one of the women, "and then see what sort of ideas God gives us."

Margaret agreed, and soon after they had finished praying, the ideas were flying.

"A florist shop from your home," said one woman. "You've always been so good at that."

"Margaret's good at anything decorative," added another lady. Jokingly she turned to Margaret and winked. "Why limit yourself to flowers? Maybe you should become an interior decorator."

Margaret started to laugh, then stopped. Was it possible? Could she actually start her own interior decorating business from her home? She was an excellent seamstress, she knew how to arrange flowers, and everyone said she had an eye for color. And it was something she loved doing. Maybe, just maybe....

Four years later, Margaret's interior decorating business is flourishing. Best of all, she's still home taking care of her little girl. And she is always very careful to give her Husband all the credit.

"He's never let me down," she proclaims. "He's always been there for me. Who could ask for a more faithful and loving Husband?"

Jordan's story is slightly different. When his wife disappeared with another man, leaving Jordan to raise their two preschoolers alone, he was terrified.

"I'd never even changed a diaper," he explained. "Well, almost never. And I had no idea what kind of food to feed my nine-month-old son. And potty training? Forget it! But I'm afraid I wasn't much better with my three-year-old. Actually, I think she survived in spite of me. I really didn't know what to do.

"We went through a string of babysitters, but it just wasn't working out. Then one day, during my personal devotions with the Lord, I came across Isaiah 54, where it says God is our Husband. I kind of laughed and said, "Gee, God, what I really need is a mother for my kids, not a husband. Would You take care of that for me too?

"The next day my sister called from Iowa. Janie's two years younger than I and had never married. She said she had been praying that morning and felt the Lord told her she was supposed to come out and stay with me for awhile and help out with the kids. I was ecstatic!

"That was almost two years ago. Janie stayed until I was able to transition into working at home—which really wasn't that difficult once I went to my boss and explained my situation. He was very cooperative in allowing me to work from home on my personal computer. Janie also helped me learn the things I needed to know to take care of my kids once she was gone. It's given me a whole new appreciation for the importance of moms—and the faithfulness of God."

As I said, God is good. Not only is He our heavenly Father, He has a mother's heart—and He is also our Husband. With a divine family like that, even the Mr. Moms of this world will find the help they need to raise their little ones successfully—no matter what Hollywood may have to say!

Don't Bother Mommy, She's Busy

Although I was 26 years old before I became a born-again Christian, I can never remember a day of my life when I didn't believe there was a God. That we could all be the result of some bizarre cosmic accident was just too ludicrous to imagine. Besides, if I accepted the premise that there was no God, then I would also have to concede that I must be more than just a little bit crazy, since I spent such a large amount of time talking to Someone who didn't exist.

Oh, I know, God doesn't answer the prayers of the unsaved, but I didn't know that then. And because I was sick so much of the time as a child and consequently spent so much time at home in bed, it seemed only natural to me that I would spend much of that time in conversation with the One I had been told was everywhere. Even though I never heard Him answer me, it comforted me to think that He was listening.

But I must admit, there was one thing about prayer that concerned me. As I said, I had heard that God was every-where, that He could do anything, and that He knew every-thing. I didn't doubt that, but what I couldn't figure out was how He could possibly pay attention to everyone at once. Surely I wasn't the only one in the world praying to Him. How could He sort through all the requests coming in at the same time? How could He tell who was asking for what? I would try to visualize what it must be like to have thousands of people talking to Him all at once, and I decided that there just had to be times when God was either too busy trying to keep all the prayers straight, or too busy trying to get them all answered.

Now, of course, I know better. God is never too busy for us—ever. He is always there. He never leaves or forsakes us, never gets confused by an inordinate number of simultaneous requests, never throws up His hands in frustration and cries out, "That's it! I just can't take one more prayer. I've had it! Leave me alone! I need a break!"

But you know what? Moms do. Lots of times. And that's okay, because we're not God. We live in a broken world with frustrations, temptations, pressures, and demands coming at us every single day. It's normal to "lose it" once in awhile. Besides, children can be very forgiving. That same child who one minute is staring up at you wide-eyed as you rant and rave over the Kool-Aid he has just spilled on your freshly mopped kitchen floor will eagerly throw his arms around you in forgiveness the moment you apologize for acting like a crazy woman.

As I said, this is normal. But it is not normal when "losing it once in awhile" becomes a way of life, when that child is afraid to come home because of the verbal and/or physical abuse he knows he will receive there.

Sadly, this sort of thing happens all too often. We've all been touched by it to some degree or another, if only through reading heartrending accounts in the newspaper. But I want to discuss a different kind of abuse, an abuse you seldom read about in newspapers, yet it is an abuse that leaves long-term emotional scars on its tiny victims. It is the abuse caused by the emotionally absent mother.

Louetta was a prime example. With her husband and three daughters, Louetta lived across the street from us in the quiet, lower-middle-class neighborhood where I grew up. Louetta's middle daughter, Betty, was my age, and we occasionally played together, but she seldom invited me to her home. The few times she did, her mother would either be locked away in her bedroom or sitting in the darkened, drapery-drawn living room watching soap operas on television. Although Louetta might glance up at us when we walked in, she never spoke to us, nor did Betty make any effort to speak to her mother. I saw no interaction between them, no expressions of love or concern or caring, scarcely even an acknowledgment of existence.

And yet Betty and her sisters were well cared for. Their clothes were always clean and neat, they seemed well-fed, and they never came home to an empty house. Mom was always there—physically. But emotionally, I doubt she ever made a connection with her daughters.

Did Louetta's emotional absenteeism have any serious effects on Betty and her sisters? Well, I have no proof, but I can tell you this: In all the years I knew Betty, I never heard her laugh. And within a timespan of less than three years, before any of the girls turned 18, one by one they all left home to get married—searching, I'm sure, for the love they had never received from their mother.

In *Always Daddy's Girl*, Norm Wright, well-known author and marriage and family counselor, states that "what a father *gives* to his daughter affects her expectations toward the men in her life. Similarly, what a father *withholds* from his daughter can also affect her expectations toward other men."[1] Author Heather Harpham agrees. In *Daddy, Where Were You?* she talks about "daughters who struggled to relate well with men, to trust God, to stop searching in all the wrong places for what they failed to receive from their dads," and "daughters who needed to find another father in God."[2]

As I have stated before, I do not discount the vital importance of a close father-child relationship—whether that child is a daughter or a son—if ever there is to be a healthy understanding of God as Father. But as I have previously stated, God the Father also has a mother's heart, and only a mother can impart to her child the understanding of the love that flows from that mother-heart.

Perhaps one of the saddest statements I have ever read was made by Sir Winston Churchill when he said about his mother, "She shone for me like the Evening Star. I loved her dearly—but at a distance."

Poignant. Heartbreaking. What it must do to a child to have to love his mother "at a distance." Certainly it cannot be what the Creator had in mind when He ordained the family unit as a place of safety and nurturing, an earthly example of the heavenly Father's Secret Place to which He calls all His children.

And yet, day after day, year after year, generation after generation, love-starved children yearn to be drawn unto their mother's bosom, only to be held at arm's length, as Louetta did to Betty and her sisters.

But not all emotionally absent mothers are as extreme in their behavior as Louetta.

Marilyn believes she is a good mother. In fact, she works quite hard at it. She is up promptly at 6:00 A.M. every morning, fixing a nourishing breakfast for her husband and two children. No one in her family ever wakes up in the morning wondering if there are clean clothes to wear or whether their lunches have been expertly packed in recyclable paper bags. In fact, they know that Mom will be standing at the front door as they leave for the day, ready to hand them those expertly packed lunches and plant a cool and proper kiss on their upturned cheeks. And while they're gone, they know that Mom will be busy cleaning and scrubbing and washing and ironing and gardening, maybe even baking their favorite cookies for when they come home.

Of course, Mom doesn't stay home every day. Sometimes she comes to school to work as a room mother or to help with PTA meetings. Other days she's involved in church or civic activities. But overall, Mom is a full-time homemaker who takes her job quite seriously.

So what's the problem? Maybe it's those cool, crisp, very proper kisses on the cheek—the only type the children have ever received from their mother. Or maybe it's the stiff, halfhearted hugs she gives them as a reward when they've accomplished something exceptionally outstanding. Because, apart from that, Marilyn does not believe in showing her children any affection whatsoever.

"It isn't that I don't love them," she explains. "It's simply that I don't want them to think it's okay to misbehave or to settle for anything less than doing their very best. That's why I'm very careful about how I dole out my affection to them, especially if they've done something wrong. If I hug and kiss them indiscriminately, they'll think it's okay to be bad, that I love them no matter what, and then they'll never learn to be all they can be."

Did you catch that? "They'll think I love them *no matter what*." Isn't that the way a mother is supposed to love her children? Isn't that the way God loves us? Of course it is! God's greatest and supreme act of love came when we were at our very worst: "But God demonstrates His own love toward us, in that *while we were still sinners*, Christ died for us" (Romans 5:8, italics mine).

Christ died for us. Not because we were good. Not because we were worthy. Not because we deserved it. Not even because we had come to Him and said we were sorry, since He died for us "while we were still sinners" and had not yet repented of our sins. He did it simply because He loved us. And because He loved us, He "demonstrates His love toward us" by giving of Himself.

Marilyn thought she was demonstrating love toward her children by the many things she did for them, but she didn't understand what God so clearly expressed through the life and death of His Son: Our loving is not demonstrated by busyness, but by giving of ourselves. And we do it *no matter what*. Then and only then do our children begin to lay hold of the depth and power of the love that flows from God's own mother-heart.

How tragic that Marilyn's children—and countless others like them—grow up believing they can only receive love when they have done something to earn it. And how tragic for Marilyn, who believes she is working so hard at being a good mother when in reality she is teaching her children just the opposite of what she is supposed to teach them as a mother: that God's love can never be earned, but can only be received as the free gift that it is. God's love and grace and forgiveness will indeed be a difficult concept for Marilyn's children to grasp.

I am also concerned about Marilyn's grandchildren. Although some children resolve to raise their own offspring in a way that is markedly different from that of their own upbringing, most go on to parent as they were parented. It is a cycle we see repeated time and time again. Child abusers were themselves usually abused as children. Children who grow up without open demonstrations of love and affection tend to perpetuate that tragedy with their own children.

Dr. Brenda Hunter in her book *Home by Choice* found that the women she interviewed who enjoyed staying at home and mothering their children were "conventional women who idealized mothering and thought positively about their own mothers." She also states that "for a woman to view motherhood positively, she needs to have been well-nurtured as a child. Otherwise, she has no reservoir of parental love to draw from for the next generation."[3]

Dr. Hunter's study of three famous feminists who have been quite vocal in their criticism of women's traditional roles as wife, mother, and homemaker—Betty Friedan, Germaine Greer, and Gloria Steinem—all turned up very negative relationships with their own mothers. You can't help but wonder how differently these three influential women might have felt toward the issue of feminism had their own mothers raised them within the biblical guidelines of family and motherhood.

Sadly, they didn't, and countless women have been swayed by the three women's feminist doctrines. Many of the women influenced by the feminist movement have left home physically and returned to the workplace. Others have stayed home physically but left emotionally, feeling as if they've been cheated simply because they were born female. But, as we saw in a previous chapter, the growing dissatisfaction of women in the workplace and their desire to return home proves that an outside job or career is not the "cure-all" that women had hoped it would be.

Janelle learned that the hard way.

"I got married during my senior year of college," Janelle explained. "I went on to graduate, but by that time I was pregnant, so I never really did anything with my diploma except hang it on the wall. By the time the women's movement was in full swing in the '70s, I had been raising kids for almost ten years. And, to tell you the truth, the thought of going out into the career world and doing something different and exciting was very appealing to me. The more I heard and read about the feminists, the more sure I became that they were right.

"I decided I was going to take that old college diploma off the wall and go out and use it! But when I announced my decision to my husband, he thought I was crazy. He asked me what I thought the kids would do while I was off working all day. I told him I'd get a sitter for after school and summer vacations. He wanted to know who would do all the cooking and cleaning around the house. I assured him that I was perfectly capable of handling all that in the evenings and on weekends. Grudgingly, he agreed. Deep down I'm sure he thought I'd never even find anything, let alone stick with it.

"He was wrong. Within a month I had landed an executive position in a bank, and the first thing I did was go out and buy a briefcase. I know that sounds kind of silly now, but at the time I thought it was a big deal. I was a bit nervous about starting a career in my mid-thirties, but I was determined to be successful.

"Was I? Well, I guess that depends on your definition of 'successful.' I did well at the bank, earning a promotion and a sizable raise in less than a year. But I soon learned it was a physical impossibility to work and still maintain my house the way I had before I got my job. I tried getting my husband and kids to pitch in, but half the time it was more trouble than it was worth to nag them about it, and I usually ended up redoing things for them anyway. So I hired a housekeeper. That helped a little, but I still had to come home and cook dinner, which I dreaded, since all I wanted to do after a long day at the office was kick off my shoes and sit down to read the paper. And of course my husband and kids always seemed to have so much to discuss with me in the evenings that I never had any time to myself to relax and unwind. I gave up trying to help the kids with their homework, assuming they were old enough by then to get it done by themselves.

"I was wrong. By the time my son hit his teens, he was flunking out of school and had been arrested twice for possession of marijuana. My daughter and I hardly speak except to argue. And I feel like I don't even know my husband anymore. He has his career and I have mine. Little comfort when that seems to be all we have left."

Brenda, on the other hand, did not go out to join the work force, even though she too was strongly influenced by the feminist movement.

"I was afraid," she admits. "Part of me wanted to go out and find a job and hopefully some fulfillment in my life. But the other part of me just didn't have the nerve. I got married right out of high school and had no job training or experience whatsoever. All I'd ever done was change diapers and wipe up messes. I didn't figure there was much call for that, but I was convinced that was all I was qualified to do. And so I stayed home and sulked. I became a soap opera addict, withdrawing completely from my husband

and children. In fact, I withdrew from reality entirely. I fantasized about how my life could have been if I hadn't gotten married and had kids, if I'd gone on to college and become some sort of professional. I was well on my way to becoming a bitter, lonely, middle-aged woman.

"And then I met Judith. Judith's family moved in next door to us when my kids were in their teens. By that time I was pretty much living in a permanent state of depression and self-pity. I had little or no interest in meeting my new neighbor, but Judith was a difficult person to avoid. Within a week of moving into her new house, she was knocking on my front door. I'll never forget that first meeting.

" 'Hi,' she said, her blue eyes sparkling with a joy that was almost offensive to me. 'I'm your new neighbor, Judith Stuart. I don't know anyone in the neighborhood and I noticed that you seem to be home during the day, so I thought I'd come over and introduce myself. I hope you don't mind.'

"I did mind, but for some strange reason I decided to let her in anyway. As I put on a fresh pot of coffee, Judith asked if I attended a church nearby. I immediately felt myself becoming defensive, and wondered if she was some kind of religious nut. When I told her I had never attended church and had no desire to start now, she just smiled and started telling me how she had not been a churchgoing person, either, until a few years earlier when she 'met Jesus Christ.'

"That's when I panicked. I knew for sure she was a religious nut then, and I was wishing I had never let her into my house, never even answered the front door. In fact, I was wishing she had never moved into our neighborhood at all! I wanted to run out of the room, to put my hands over my ears to drown out her words—but I just couldn't. Deep down inside me there was something just crying out to know about and share in the joy that I saw on her face.

"By the time we finished that pot of coffee, Judith and I had prayed together and I too had met Jesus Christ. I knew at that moment that my life would never be the same. The depression, the anxiety, the self-pity—all of it was gone. I'd found something that no job or career in all the world could ever have given me. I'd found peace and love and contentment. And I'd found forgiveness and release from the bitterness that had been choking the life out of me for so many years.

"Now Judith and I go to church together. My family hasn't joined me yet, but I'm believing that they will. Already they've seen such a change in me that they've begun to ask questions about Jesus Christ and His plan of salvation. For now they're happy just to see me at peace and with a purpose for my life.

"That's what it's all about, you know. You can't find that peace and purpose anywhere else. I just pray that mothers everywhere—those who stay at home and those who go out to work every day—will discover that truth, as I have. Nothing could be better."

Whether your children come home to a physically absent mother or an emotionally absent one, the answer is still the same—Jesus Christ. He is the only One who can fill that vacuum within, the only One who brings peace and contentment and joy. And once we have that, we have everything we need to nurture and raise our children as the mother-heart of God longs for us to do. Because God, you see—unlike mothers—never gets too busy or too tired or too inundated with requests. He always has time for us, and He always loves us.

It may have taken me 26 years to learn that, but I will never forget it.

The Sandwich Mommy

When Faye had her third child in less than four years, she thought she was just about as busy as any one woman could ever be.

"There were times I was sure I was destined to change diapers for the rest of my life," she recalls. "I'd forgotten what a decent night's sleep or a neat and tidy house was like. And I'd long since given up on ever finding any spare time for myself. There just never seemed to be enough hours in the day to do everything that needed to be done.

"By the time the kids hit their teens, I thought I was home free. And then Dad died. That's when I *really* learned the meaning of the word 'busy.'"

Like many women in this country, Faye, already a busy wife and mother, joined the ranks of "sandwich mommies"—women who care for both children and aging parents—when her father died and her mother came to live with them.

"It seemed like the perfect solution at the time," she explains. "I mean, I certainly couldn't leave Mom alone in that big house, especially with the problems she was already experiencing with Alzheimer's. Dad had taken care of her for so long, but when he died suddenly, I never even considered any other options. I insisted Mom come home to live with us, and that was that. Now, after two years of stretching my role as caretaker for my very active teenage children to include caretaker for my mother, I can't help but wonder if we wouldn't all have been better off if I had at least checked into some alternatives before making such a rash decision."

Faye's case is not an isolated one. As a result of improved health care and overall health consciousness, Americans are living longer these days. As a result, grown children often find themselves in the position of helping to care for their aged parents. In fact, it is said that "today's parents will spend approximately 17 years caring for their children— but the children will spend 18 years caring for their parents."[1] And, no matter how you cut it, when we say that "today's parents" will be the caretakers, what we actually mean is that the already busy woman in the family is probably going to be shouldering the lion's share of the actual physical caretaking.

"A caregiver may be a spouse, an adult daughter or son, a relative, a friend, a neighbor—you or me," says author Ruth Bathauer in her book *Parent Care*. "Families, like individuals, are unique; therefore, there is a great variety in the way each family chooses the caregiver. Professionals in the field of family relations generally agree that, no matter how many adult children are in a family, the responsibility of caring for dependent parents usually falls to the women. It may be the oldest daughter who has children of her own, the youngest daughter who may still live at home with her parents, or even a daughter-in-law."

Bathauer goes on to say, "Research shows that 80 percent of caregivers are the female adult children. Even when aging parents have an only son, the caregiver is usually the daughter-in-law."[2]

So here we have an additional burden to heap on top of the already overburdened, double-duty wife and mother of today. As Faye exclaimed, "Good grief! As busy as I am with a house, a husband, three teenagers, and a semi-invalid mother, I can't imagine what I'd do if I had to juggle an outside career on top of all that! Oh no, it would never work."

And yet some women are doing just that. Connie, for instance, is a nurse with a rotating shift, two children in elementary school, a husband who is on the road a lot because of his job, and a blind father-in-law who lives with them "because we just couldn't bear the thought of putting him anywhere else.

"But it's hard," Connie admits. "Very hard. Pop lost his eyesight in a work-related accident just before he retired. He became very bitter and refused therapy or training to learn to cope with his disability. When my mother-in-law died, we knew we couldn't leave Pop alone, even though he insisted that's what he wanted. He grudgingly came to live with us so we could take care of him, but he has never stopped complaining—about everything! He complains about being alone so much, especially when I'm gone to work, about the woman we hired to come in and care for him when we're gone, about the noise the kids make, about my cooking.

"Sometimes I think I look forward to going to work just so I can get away from him for awhile—which adds a feeling of guilt to everything else. But I think the hardest thing is the growing tension between Pop and the kids. At an age when they should be enjoying each other, all they do is get on one another's nerves. To tell you the truth, it doesn't do a whole lot for my nerves, either. It's hard enough to balance my wife and mother responsibilities with my job, without this additional problem. But we just don't know what else to do.

"Sometimes I feel like throwing my hands up in the air and running out the door—for good! You know, leave everything behind—all of it! I know I'll never do that, of course, but sometimes it seems to be the only way I'll ever find any time for myself.

"But the worst part," continues Connie, "is feeling like there just isn't enough of me to go around. No matter how hard I try, it's just never enough."

Never enough of me to go around. What a sad but common lament among countless women—women who have been caught up in that "Superwoman" syndrome we discussed in an earlier chapter. First, these women want to be good wives and mothers, as well as successful career women. Then, when an aging, ailing parent needs care, they feel compelled to offer it, never taking into account the possible ramifications for all concerned.

Hence the "sandwich mommy" is pressed in on all sides until she feels her very life is being squeezed right out of her.

"Caregiving can be physically and emotionally exhausting," warns Bathauer in her book, advising that not all women are capable of caring for aging parents, particularly if the parent is disabled or incapacitated in some way. If, however, you find yourself in a situation where you are faced with the possibility of taking your aging parent into your home, here are some factors to consider:

- How has your relationship been with your parent(s) over the years? Do you communicate well? Is there a sense of mutual respect? Do your lifestyles mesh, or do you have little in common?

- How does the rest of your family feel about the situation? This is never a decision that should be made without the unanimous support of everyone within the household.

- Who will be the primary caretaker? If there is a medical problem, does that primary caretaker have the training and/or ability to handle difficult situations that may arise? If not, are funds available to hire someone to deal with this aspect of caretaking?

- Is your parent going to be happy with this situation? Would it be more appropriate for your parent to be in a situation with others of the same age?

- Have you honestly considered and explored other options? Within your parent's financial capabilities, is there another situation that might better suit the needs of all concerned?

- Most important, have you asked the Lord to show you your true motive in bringing your parent into your home? If you make this decision based on any reason other than knowing that it is God's will for you and your family (i.e., a false sense of guilt, fulfilling your own needs, a belief that it is the "Christian thing to do," etc.), you will only compound the problem, not solve it.

These are some hard questions, but questions that need to be answered before making any life-changing decisions. Whether you are a career mom or a stay-at-home mom, you are undoubtedly living with a full schedule. Would bringing your parent into your home at this point be a positive move, or would it exacerbate an already tension-filled situation?

"That's what happened to me," explains Evelyn. "Even though my mother and I had always had an excellent relationship, when Dad died and we brought Mom home to live with us, our relationship changed for the worse.

"It wasn't really too bad at first," Evelyn went on. "Oh, you know, there were a few minor things, like getting used to someone else in my kitchen, learning not to take offense at her suggestions about my housekeeping or child-rearing—things like that. But in other ways it was kind of nice, especially the fact that she was there to greet the kids when they got home from school or stay with them if they were home sick. I always felt so bad about being a latchkey mother, but with our finances the way they were, we didn't feel we had a choice. So in that respect Mom's being there was a real plus.

"But then she fell and broke her hip. When she came home from the hospital, her insurance paid for a nurse's aide to come in for a few hours during the day, but in the evenings, after a long day at work, I had to take over.

"Now don't get me wrong. It wasn't that I didn't want to help. I love my mother dearly, and I felt terrible about her accident. But I'm a lousy nurse, and Mom's a lousy patient. She was critical and demanding, I was cranky and resentful, and before you knew it our relationship was deteriorating right before our eyes.

"Thankfully, my husband was wise enough to see the strain it was putting on the whole family. He called a family meeting and we all sat down—including the kids—and discussed things openly. We didn't come up with a solution right away, but eventually we decided that the best thing for everyone was for Mom to move to a retirement center a few miles away. It was a lovely place, with people her own age to visit with, and loads of fun activities. Besides that, they had 24-hour care if she ever needed it. And it was close enough that we could all visit once or twice a week.

"It was perfect. Because it was a mutual decision, I didn't feel guilty about Mom going there. And what a relief to have that one added pressure off my shoulders! In no time Mom and I were back to the close relationship we had shared for so many years."

A retirement home is an option that may not be open to everyone, since many of them are quite expensive. But others charge according to the individual's income. The advantage of this type of living is that it helps the elderly maintain their independence and self-respect, while still providing whatever care may be necessary.

Retirement homes, however, usually will not take new residents who are already invalids or seriously disabled. Rest homes and special-need homes would be better suited to these situations.

But if none of these options are available, maybe one obvious possibility is being overlooked here. Is it possible that the best solution for some aging parents is to have them continue to live alone for as long as possible? So many of the adult children I spoke with said they had "insisted" their parent come to live with them, only to find that unexpected problems arose later. I wonder if they ever considered that some of those problems might have been a result of the fact that the parent would have preferred living alone but went along with the move to please the insistent adult child.

According to a report from the National Center for Health, many senior citizens prefer living alone, even after the death of a spouse. And, depending on health and/or physical and mental capabilities, there's really no reason why they shouldn't continue to do so as long as possible. If you are concerned about your parent's welfare while living alone, different levels of home assistance are available, ranging from someone who checks in with your parent on regular intervals to full-time, live-in care. In some communities, adult day health-care centers are also an option.

Of course, even with all these options available, there are occasions when you may feel you simply have no choice but to take your parent into your home.

If that becomes the case, then it is important to first take stock of the rest of your home situation: Are you already working away from home? If so, are you doing so out of financial need or simply because you want to do so? Can you handle the conflicting pressures of homemaker, career woman, and "sandwich mommy"?

If not, what changes can you make? Can the parent coming into your home be of some help with childcare and/or housework, cooking, shopping, etc.? Is your career something you can give up or scale back to take off some of the pressure? Because if you can't cut back on existing pressure, adding more pressure to the situation could be disastrous to your family life. Those little ones who wait all day at the daycare for you to come home and spend some time with them are not going to appreciate your spending that time with your parent instead. Are you already feeling like there's not enough of you to go around? What are you going to do if you have to spread yourself even thinner?

For the woman who already feels she is being pressured into doing double-duty as both homemaker and bread-winner, adding to her caretaker duties is only going to create more resentment. When that happens, nobody wins.

Mom's pressure level is going to be on overload. When that happens, she's going to be snapping at everyone around her, but feeling terribly guilty for doing so. There will be less time in an already crowded schedule for Dad and the kids. And if it's all being done with the idea of doing the aging parent a favor, forget it. Grandma or Grandpa isn't going to be any happier living in that kind of an environment than anyone else.

In addition to unconditional love and the meeting of physical needs, the one thing an aging parent needs most is to retain his or her dignity. This is difficult at best, particularly when being taken care of by a dutiful but obviously resentful adult child.

Virginia was heartbroken when her mother's stroke left her unable to do most of the things she had loved for so many years. Although her mother's mind was still clear, she had trouble communicating and was partially paralyzed. With good intentions, Virginia took her mother into her home to care for her, telling herself that the warning signal she felt inside would fade in time.

It didn't. In fact, the signal sounded louder and louder with each passing day. As Virginia rushed home from work every day, picking up her son, Tommy, from the babysitter on the way, the knot in her stomach grew. By the time she got home and walked into her mother's room to relieve the visiting nurse's aide, Virginia's heart felt as if it would pound right out of her chest. There was just so much to do!

Dinner, dishes, Tommy's homework, helping her mom eat, visiting with her, helping her get ready for bed—not to mention spending at least a token amount of time with her husband.

It was impossible. But Virginia just wouldn't admit it. She grew more and more impatient and resentful toward her mother, and her tone of voice reflected it. One evening as Virginia berated her mother for spilling her applesauce, the older woman began to cry.

"Not...a child," she sobbed, struggling to be understood. "Don't...treat me like...a child."

Virginia's heart was broken. Is that what she had been doing? Treating her mother like a child, rather than giving her the love and respect she deserved?

That's when Virginia sought help. First she talked to her husband, who admitted to having had misgivings about the situation all along. Together they went to their pastor, who listened to their story in amazement.

"And you wonder why you're reacting like this?" he asked Virginia incredulously. "It's a wonder you haven't broken completely."

Virginia shook her head. "But...but I thought...well, since I'm a Christian, shouldn't I be able to handle this? Isn't this what the Bible teaches, that we should honor our parents?"

"Of course we're to honor our parents," the pastor replied gently. "But do you think you're honoring your mother the way things are right now? Virginia, the Bible promises that God will not put more on us than we can bear, but it doesn't promise that we won't do that to ourselves. It sounds to me like you've taken on a lot more than God ever intended you to."

Virginia's eyes opened wide. "You mean...I shouldn't have taken Mom home to live with us?"

"I can't answer that," he replied. "But I can tell you this: Taking your mother into your home is not something you should have done without much prayer first—and the total support of the rest of your family."

Virginia and her husband exchanged glances, then she looked back at her pastor. Her voice was quiet when she spoke. "I'm...I'm going to have to make some sort of change, aren't I?"

"That's for you and your family to discuss," he answered, "*and* pray about. You do that, and you won't have to ask me what to do. You'll already know."

By the end of the week her pastor's words had come to pass. "I've decided to quit my job," Virginia announced when she and her husband next met with their pastor.

The pastor raised his eyebrows. "That's a major decision," he observed.

"Yes," Virginia admitted, "but I know it's the right one—for now, anyway. I finally admitted that I just can't do it all—the house, the job, my family, and now my mom too. And we all really want Mom to stay. So for now the job goes on the back burner." She leaned back in her chair and smiled. "And you know what? After all that wrestling to come to this decision, it feels so good to finally have made it. What a relief! And that knot in my stomach is finally gone.

"You were right," she went on. "It wasn't God putting all these stresses and pressures on me—I was doing it to myself! I was trying so hard to be Superwoman, and all I was accomplishing—at least, according to my son—was being Supergrouch!"

Virginia laughed. "Not anymore!" she vowed. "The pressure's off, and now I'm just going to enjoy my family, including my mom. Now that I'm not so tired and crabby all the time, I can treat her with the love and respect she deserves—and that's what honoring my parents is really all about, isn't it?"

That's what it's all about, Virginia—treating your parents with the love and respect they deserve, in whatever way best fits your individual situation. And the only way to be sure of finding out that best way for you and your family is to consult—and obey—the heavenly Father with the mother's heart—the One who never puts more on us than we can bear.

What's a Mom to Do?

CHAPTER 7

Time and again throughout this book we have touched on the idea of the mother-heart of God. We've also discussed the fact that it is not a "Good Mommy/Bad Mommy" issue we are up against here, but rather a master deceiver who is out to destroy families, combined with a society that would convince us that social parenting is the wave of the future. We have examined the fallout of a generation of children growing up crying, "I want my Mommy!" but getting no response, as well as the "Mr. Mom" and single-parenting issue, the emotionally absent mother, and the "sandwich mommy." So now that we've identified the problems, what's the answer? In other words, *what's a mom to do?*

In this chapter we will not discuss financial options at great length, since we will be examining that issue in more detail in the next chapter. However, I believe that if we're going to get any clear-cut direction on how to deal with the situation of mother-hungry children, we're going to have to get real serious about our study of God's proper parenting manual, the Bible.

Colossians 3:2 is, I believe, the starting point for setting up our priorities in a way that will line up with God's instructions for parenting. This verse tells us, "Set your mind on things above, not on things on the earth." Pastor

E.V. Hill is famous for preaching a sermon based on this verse. He calls it "This ain't it!" Yes, we know that "this ain't it," but do we live like we believe it?

The mindset of the world is that we only go around once, so we might as well go for all the gusto we can get—and pity anyone who tries to get in our way! But I wonder how many of us who name the name of Jesus as Lord and Savior live much differently.

Our Lord taught us that if we are willing to daily give up our lives for His sake, our lives will be saved; if we seek to hang on to them, they will be lost. It is a daily cross we are told to pick up and carry if we are to follow after Him. It is a daily dying to self in order that we might live in Him, and pass that life on to others. And who do we most want to see that life passed on to but our children? What greater legacy can we possibly leave them? But do you truly think our children are going to be convinced that following Jesus is the way to go when they see us heading in the opposite direction?

Yet that's exactly what we're doing when we allow ourselves to be pressed into the mold of the world. Romans 12:2 warns us, "Do not be conformed to this world, but be transformed by the renewing of your mind, that you may prove what is that good and acceptable and perfect will of God." It is the world that tells us we must have a career if we are to be fulfilled. It is the world that tells us we must make more money to buy a bigger house and drive a newer car and wear nicer clothes. It is the world that tells us that who we are is determined by what we have and how hard we're working in order to get more and more and more.

Jesus says, "But seek first the kingdom of God and His righteousness, and all these things shall be added to you" (Matthew 6:33). What is it we are truly seeking? Are we seeking God, desiring to know and love and please Him above all else, and trusting Him to supply our needs accordingly? Or are we allowing the world system to press us into its mold, conforming us to its image instead of allowing God to transform us into the image of His Son?

The choice is ours. God has given us a free will, first to decide if we will follow Him at all, and then, even after we have been born into His family, to decide to what extent we will honor and serve Him.

The problem is that we have too many Christians who are satisfied with nothing more than fire insurance. They have been born again and they know they're going to heaven, but they don't want to pay the price to live for God here on earth. The tragedy in that decision is the negative impact it has on those around them, especially their children. Young people are basically idealistic and self-righteous. They can spot a hypocrite a mile away. If they hear us talking about serving Jesus with our lips, but see us serving the devil and the world system with our actions, we will succeed only in driving them away from Christianity rather than toward it.

Think about it: Is it important to you for your children to see you worshiping your career, throwing all your time and energy and devotion into material success? Do you want your children to model that lifestyle? Because they very well may. And if they do, you may someday find that you have some very successful children—financially and materialistically speaking, that is. But what did Jesus say in Mark 8:36? "For what will it profit a man if he gains the whole world, and loses his own soul?" Would you rather have your child serving the Lord with all his heart regardless of his social or economic status, or reveling in the world's success while giving no thought or consideration to his eternal destiny?

It all comes back to that crucial matter of priorities. And sometimes—most of the time—right priorities require personal sacrifice. That's a tough and extremely unpopular message to preach in this "me-first, I-want-it-all-and-I-want-it-now" generation. But that same mindset that drives a young criminal to rob or sell drugs to satisfy his immediate cravings is what drives us to work more and buy more and charge what we can't afford so we don't have to do without or wait until we can afford it. The bottom line is, we've forgotten what E.V. Hill said: "This ain't it!"

This world and all that we can see with our eyes is going to pass away. Jesus says we "are not of the world, just as I am not of the world" (John 17:16). And yet we throw ourselves into the life of this world as if it were going to last forever.

Think about it: The Bible teaches that as Christians we have three enemies: the world, the flesh, and the devil—and the three of them work hand in hand to destroy us.

Let's talk about these enemies for a moment. The first enemy mentioned is the world. What is meant here by "world" is the entire system over which the devil maintains influence and control. It is a system, a kingdom, that works in direct opposition to God's kingdom. The world system, Satan's domain, demands its rights and disdains its responsibilities. It seeks only its own, honors only itself, and worships no god other than self. And that is why it is doomed to destruction.

The principles of God's kingdom, however, are just the opposite. God calls us to "esteem others better than" ourselves (see Philippians 2:3); to love in such a way that we seek other people's good, no matter the cost to self; and to "have no other gods" (Exodus 20:3) except our heavenly Father—the One with the mother-heart.

The god of this world—the devil—is another of our three enemies. Just the fact that he is the god of a world system that is in total opposition to the kingdom of God is proof enough that he is out to destroy us. But the thing we must remember is that Satan's chief tool of destruction is deception.

From the beginning, Satan has used deception to destroy God's people. In the Garden of Eden he lied to Eve and told her that if she ate of the tree of the knowledge of good and evil she would not die. Obviously he is a skillful liar, because she believed him. Since that day the deceiver has been working overtime. Revelation 12:9 tells us that "Satan...deceives the whole world." Everyone who is not a born-again believer is living under Satan's deceptive sway. If this were not so, they would believe the gospel and be saved, because Jesus is the truth (see John 14:6). To reject Jesus Christ is to reject the truth, and therefore continue living in deception.

But Satan's time and energy do not go into deceiving the world, since he already has them. The ones he is working so hard to deceive are *us*, the children of God, as we see so clearly in Matthew 24:24, where Jesus discusses the end times and warns of Satan's purpose "to deceive, if possible, even the elect."

The elect are us, the church, those who have been born again and assured of a home in heaven. Satan knows he cannot steal our salvation, but he is determined to keep us from walking in victory in this life and from being effective witnesses to others. The surest way for him to do this is to keep our minds off of the truth that "this ain't it"! So long as we are blinded and deceived into thinking that what's important are the things of this world (Satan's domain), the devil's job will be an easy one. Contrary to the command we read earlier in Colossians 3:2, our minds will be set on things on the earth rather than on things above, where our permanent home awaits us.

And then there is the third enemy—the flesh. I don't know about you, but this is the one I least like to discuss. The reason, of course, is because it's the one I have the most trouble with. Oh, I'd like to blame all my problems and shortcomings (should I just be honest and call them "sins"?) on the world or the devil, but the truth is that "the spirit indeed is willing, but the flesh is weak" (Matthew 26:41). I want to serve the Lord, I want to live for Him, I want to take up my cross daily and follow Him, I want to decrease so He can increase in my life, but that old flesh of mine fights me every step of the way.

And you know what? You can't bind it, curse it, or cast it out. You can't ignore it, deny its existence, or wish it away. Even the apostle Paul admitted this when he said in Romans 7:22,23, "I delight in the law of God according to the inward man. But I see another law in my members, warring against the law of my mind, and bringing me into captivity to the law of sin which is in my members."

We all fight it, every day of our lives. And we will continue to do so until we die or until Jesus comes back for us. That's why it's such a tough battle—because it lasts so long—and that's why the devil has it so easy when he comes at us and tries to "wear out the saints" (Daniel 7:25 KJV). Even the best-intentioned saints can get worn out when they find themselves fighting the same battle day after day.

So what's the answer? There is only one, and that is to make our relationship with Jesus Christ our number one priority—no matter what! If we sense that God is calling us to rearrange our other priorities, then we must be obedient to do so, whatever the cost. If not, our three enemies—the world, the flesh, and the devil—will entice us, deceive us, and wear us down. When that happens, who will lead our children out of the darkness and into the light?

Moses was the one God used to lead the Israelites out of bondage. We as parents are the ones God wants to use to lead our children out of the bondage of serving the devil. Moses incurred ridicule and rejection from Pharaoh and the world system when he obeyed God. We may very well have to deal with some level of persecution or sacrifice ourselves when we take a stand for the things of God, but isn't our children's salvation worth any cost?

If we fail to accept God's challenge to lead our children in the right way, we shouldn't be shocked and dismayed when they choose instead to go the wrong way. When the only role models our children have to follow are those who receive honors and accolades for admitting to having contracted a deadly disease through years of promiscuous sex, should we be surprised when the youth of today follow blindly after them? When we live in a world that allows school nurses and/or counselors to assist our teenage daughters in arranging abortions without parental consent, yet those same school officials cannot dispense an aspirin to a student with a headache, should we be amazed that the confused youth of today are headed for destruction at breakneck speed?

I once saw a cartoon that was a sad commentary on this very situation. A school official is looking down at two young children. She says, "You want condoms? No problem! Just don't ask for Bibles, okay?"

The world system, headed up by the devil himself, is becoming more and more blatant every day in its attack on all that is good and right and godly. If we as Christians sell out and join this system, what hope do our children have?

At the same time, let's be honest here. We all know of families—maybe even our own—where parents are both strong believers, seeking to serve the Lord with all their heart, modeling a godly lifestyle to their children, and yet one or more of these children end up in trouble. What's the explanation?

Well, if you're looking to me for the answer, I'm not sure I can give you one. But I can say this: Children growing up in a godly home have a lot better chance of making it to adulthood emotionally, physically, and spiritually intact than those children who do not have that guidance. And even if these children do get into trouble along the way, Christian parents have a powerful means of dealing with the situation that unbelieving parents do not have. That powerful means, of course, is the presence of God in their lives. The important thing is that even if a child does get sidetracked, the parents must stand firm in what they believe God would have them do in their individual situation.

God deals differently with each of us. Although there are certain "givens" in Scripture regarding child-rearing, there are also some flexible areas where God may direct parents to deal with their children in ways unique from other parents with similar situations.

In our own case, when our youngest hit his teens, he suddenly decided that family rules no longer applied to him, and proceeded to make his own rules—which basically amounted to whatever he did or did not feel like doing at the moment. A horrendous period of fighting and bickering and frustration followed. Then, after seeking the Lord for a practical and workable solution, we drew up what has become affectionately known around our home as "The Contract."

Although my husband and son and I all sat down together and discussed the terms of that contract, the final word on what went into it was mine and my husband's. After reviewing it in detail, we all three signed and dated the document, made copies, and filed them away for "posterity"—and for the very next time a conflict arose, which wasn't very long. When my son began to argue about a certain family rule, we simply got out the contract, reread it, and settled the argument.

Now I'm not going to tell you that this arrangement has made my son a happy camper, but it has certainly restored an element of peace to our home. Most importantly, it has restored a sense of control to us, which as parents is vital for a family's survival. "The Contract," for us, has been a positive answer to a very negative and yet quite common problem—that of teenage rebellion. At this point, when my son starts to flop his big toe across the parental line, I no longer even have to dig out the contract to settle the issue. The mere mention of it is enough to elicit from my son a disgusted sigh and a roll of the eyes heavenward. Reluctantly, he backs down.

And if he doesn't? I must admit, as a mother, that was my biggest concern. Soon after the contract was signed, the issue came to a head. My son decided that one of the contract's terms was not acceptable and he simply would not abide by it. He announced that he was leaving and would just go find somewhere else to live where there weren't so many rules and regulations.

He lasted about five hours, until it got cold and dark—and he got hungry. As for myself, I spent those five hours praying and reading every promise in the Bible that I could find regarding my children. I must confess to some moments of distress, as visions of my child sleeping on the street or being mugged at knifepoint haunted me, but I knew we were taking the stand God had told us to take, and I knew God would honor that stand and bring him home safely. He did.

Of course, as I said, God deals differently with everyone. Just because He directed us to draw up a contract with our son does not necessarily mean that this is the answer for others who are experiencing problems with their teenagers. It's simply an option that is working for us.

There are other options, too, including family counseling and support groups. Tough Love is a well-known support group for parents having problems with their children, although it is not biblically based. A group of parents from our church who had previously been involved with Tough Love have broken off from them and started their own Christ-centered support group called Ray of Hope. The purpose of this group is to help "parents having problems with their children—offering active, loving support in the hope of re-establishing cooperation and sanity in the household through consistent discipline, administered with unconditional love." The group is having excellent results.

But if a support group isn't for you, you can still key in on Ray of Hope's purposes and principles. Consistent discipline and unconditional love are the mainstays in dealing with this type of situation, and must be practiced daily. But without total dependence on the love and grace and strength of God, it simply can't be done.

It all comes right back to the same thing: If we are to be effective parents, our relationship with Jesus Christ must be our top priority. Nothing less will do. Anything else would be to cheat our children of the heritage that is rightfully theirs as a result of having been born into a Christian family.

We cannot do it alone. And we certainly cannot do it the world's way. It must be God's way—the way of the heavenly Father with a mother-heart. And if that mother-heart is calling you home to be with your children, be willing to make whatever sacrifices might be necessary to answer that call.

Do it for your children. Your own mother-heart will never regret it.

Moms and Money— Getting Creative

One of the most familiar and often-quoted Scriptures in the entire Bible is Philippians 4:19, which promises, "My God shall supply all your need according to His riches in glory by Christ Jesus." Sadly, it is also one of the most misused verses of Scripture in the entire Bible.

Now don't get me wrong. I have literally clung to that verse for dear life on more than one occasion. But in doing so I learned a valuable lesson: God does meet our needs, but there are certain conditions that we must meet if we are to walk in the truth of that Scripture.

First, we must remember that "no prophecy of Scripture is of any private interpretation" (2 Peter 1:20). We cannot go through the Bible looking for a favorite verse that suits our particular situation, and then pull it out and build an entire doctrine around it. That's a real good way to get away from the truth and off into error. No, if we are to understand and appropriate the truth of a particular verse of Scripture in our lives, we must do so in light of the entire Word of God. Unfortunately, although most Christians want God to meet all their needs—particularly their financial ones—too many of those same Christians do not want to hear what the Word of God has to say about their finances.

Yes, I can hear those groans now. You think I'm going to talk about the "t" word. Well, you're right. The Bible leaves no room for argument when it comes to tithing. It is required for all believers, whether we like the idea or not. And lest you quote the old familiar argument that tithing is under the law and we are no longer under the law, let's start our examination of the validity of tithing in Genesis 14, before the law was given.

In verse 14 we see that Abram (whose name has not yet been changed to Abraham) receives news that his nephew Lot has been taken captive, so he sets out to rescue him. Not only does Abram rescue Lot, but he plunders Lot's captives and takes their goods. Then in verse 18 Abram meets Melchizedek, "king of Salem" and "the priest of God Most High."

Little is said about Melchizedek throughout Scripture; however, in prophesying about the coming Lord and Savior Psalm 110:4 declares, "You are a priest forever according to the order of Melchizedek." This same verse is quoted by the writer of Hebrews when referring to the priesthood of Christ (see Hebrews 5:6; 7:21).

What we do know about Melchizedek is that he blessed Abram, and then received from Abram "a tithe of all." If the great patriarch Abram gave to Melchizedek "a tithe of all" before the institution of the law, are we to assume that giving *at the very least* "a tithe of all" to the One who is "a priest forever according to the order of Melchizedek" is not required of us?

I say *at the very least* here because a tithe of all we have (which, no matter how you cut it, means 10 percent of everything right off the top) should be our starting place for giving to God. The first 10 percent meets our required giving—anything less, according to Malachi 3:8, is robbing God—anything over and above that is a love offering.

Why does God have it set up that way? Well, of course, I don't presume to understand God's ways, but I would venture to say it's because He knows our hearts. He knows we are, in and of ourselves, tightfisted rather than open-handed givers. If left to our own devices, we might toss a few dollars into the offering plate now and then and think we have done God a favor. What arrogance! Do we really think God needs our money? Of course not! But He knows that *we need to give.* Tithing is God's way of teaching us to become a giving people; remember, He taught us that in giving our lives away we will keep them, but in grasping them to ourselves we will certainly lose them (see Luke 9:24).

There is another great principle we must see here if we are to understand New Testament giving. Remembering that Jesus said, "Do not think that I came to destroy the Law or the Prophets. I did not come to destroy but to fulfill" (Matthew 5:17), let's turn to the fifth chapter of Matthew and examine that portion of Scripture commonly referred to as the "Sermon on the Mount."

In verses 21 and 22 of that chapter Jesus starts out by saying, "You have heard that it was said....But I say to you...." He repeats these phrases several times throughout the remainder of this chapter. What Jesus is doing here is not refuting the Old Testament law, but rather showing that to fulfill it requires a heart obedience, not just an outward compliance. He is teaching His listeners that, to be His disciples, they must go beyond that which was required of them by religious ordinances; they must be cheerful givers (see 2 Corinthians 9:7), giving over and above what is required of them simply because they love God and know that all they have is His anyway.

So if the example in Genesis 14 of Abram tithing to Melchizedek prior to the establishment of the law isn't enough to convince you that tithing is more than a requirement of the law, then go ahead and believe that tithing was just for Old Testament times. But since we now live in New Testament times, under grace rather than under law, we must deal with the truth of Hebrews 8:6, which says, "But now He [Jesus Christ] has obtained a *more excellent ministry*, inasmuch as He is also Mediator of a *better covenant*, which was established on *better promises*" (italics mine).

If Jesus Christ has obtained a more excellent ministry, if He is the Mediator of a better covenant established on better promises, then shouldn't we who live under that better covenant with its better promises walk in a more excellent way and be better givers than those who lived under the old covenant with its lesser promises?

This brings us to only one logical conclusion: To give any less than "a tithe of all" would be to rob God; to give over and above that tithe as an act of love is to be expected of those who would call themselves disciples of the One who is the Mediator of the better covenant. These are those "certain conditions" I mentioned at the beginning of this chapter that must be met if we are to rightfully claim the promise of Philippians 4:19. To attempt to claim that promise for ourselves when we are not living within God's economic principles is as ludicrous as trying to claim God's protection when we have walked out from under that umbrella of protection by continuing in unconfessed sin. It just doesn't work.

At the same time, I know there are many women in positions where they are unable to tithe, simply because they may be married to an unbeliever or even to a believer who does not practice tithing. If this is the case, remember that God knows your heart. He knows whether or not you would tithe if you could, so if this is truly the case—and not just an excuse because you really don't want to tithe—you can still trust in God's promise to provide for your needs.

Now I know that tithing is a hard subject to discuss, and certainly not a popular one. But I felt it necessary to lay the groundwork first before going on to discuss creative solutions to everyday financial pressures. Because if we're not going to obey God when it comes to tithes and offerings, all the other money management ideas are worthless.

However, if you have already decided that you are going to be obedient in what God has called you to regarding His first principle of wise stewardship—more commonly known as money management—then let's move on to some other suggestions that I believe will be helpful in resolving the "Must-I-go-out-to-work-or-can-I-possibly-find-some-way-to-stay-home-with-my-children" issue.

Let's deal first with the mothers who are working to bring in a second income. Many of them feel they are in a financial situation in which they have no choice. But remember the example of the hypothetical clerical worker in Chapter 4? She started out with a salary of $350 per week; after taking out her expenses, she ended up with a net profit of about $85. Is it worth it to you to go out to work every day and leave your children with babysitters or in daycare centers just so you can contribute an extra $85 per week to the family budget? If not, let's look at some creative ways of making at least that much money while staying at home.

The first and most obvious way is by saving that amount through wise budgeting and thrifty shopping. It is amazing to me how many women run to the store several times a week to pick up "a few odds and ends." Do you know that you can cut your grocery budget by 25 to 50 percent simply by shopping for larger quantities less often? Why pay $1.98 for a small jar of peanut butter that may not last a week when you can buy an economy-sized jar that will last all month for only $3.98? By watching for sales, a mere 30 cents can mean the difference between a package of spaghetti large enough for three meals instead of just one.

And doesn't it make sense to cut back on the number of trips to the store each week? Not only will it reduce your gasoline bill, but as busy as most of us are, I should think we would appreciate that extra time we save by not going to the store every day. Oh, I know, you may still have to run back and pick up a gallon of milk once in awhile, but discipline yourself to grab the milk and go, rather than browsing and picking up "bargains" that you really don't need.

Speaking of bargains, the food displays at the end of the aisles are very often not your best buys. Don't yield to impulse buying just because an item is hyped as a great deal. Compare these "come-ons" with similar items before tossing them into your shopping cart.

And then there are coupons. Ah, yes, one of the joys of my life! I must admit, I'm just weird enough that I actually get excited when I open the Sunday paper and see all those coupons just waiting to be clipped. But even coupon use deserves a word of caution. Although you can legitimately save a bundle using them, they can also suck you into buying things you really don't need or even want. Don't buy three boxes of Super-Sugar Frooties Cereal just because you can save 40 cents on each box. Do you have any idea how long it takes to get rid of three giant-sized boxes of cereal that nobody likes? Trust me—it's a long time.

Another thing to consider before using those coupons is whether you can save even more by buying one of the store brands. True, not all store-brand items are of as high a quality as the name brands, but most are, and the price is usually substantially lower.

One of the things that drives up your grocery bill when you're out working is quick-fix foods. You know, the kind you buy when you're so tired after a long day at work that you don't want to do anything but throw a family-sized frozen pizza into the microwave. But if you haven't been out working all day, maybe you have a little more time and can buy less of the prepackaged foods. It's a sure way to save a few extra dollars each week.

But even if all these tips on cutting back expenses isn't adding up to enough difference to compensate for your staying home from work, what about bringing in a little extra income right from your own home?

In Chapter 4 we discussed a few creative ways that single parents had found to make a living from home. If single parents can do it, certainly those looking to supplement their spouse's income can do the same. Let's look at a few of those options.

The first thing that always comes to mind—and often elicits a groan or a sigh—is daycare. And yet, if you're already home with one or two of your own, what's a couple more? There's certainly a need, and other than getting a license (and possessing an inordinate amount of love and patience) it's a relatively simple enterprise to get started.

But if babysitting other people's children is not for you, start by asking yourself what it is that you enjoy doing. I once heard a panel discussion by a group of women who had started businessess out of their own home. They each said they started at the same point: They saw a need that they were able to meet and they met it by marketing what they enjoyed doing.

Cora loved to bake. When her husband, Joe, had a heart attack, the doctors put him on a low-cholesterol diet. Suddenly they had to change all their eating habits. Cora's pies and cakes and cookies were off-limits. But Joe still wanted something "yummy," and Cora still wanted to bake. So she started to experiment with cholesterol-free goodies. She did so well that she began to pass some on to her neighbor, whose husband had also been advised to cut back on cholesterol.

"I checked the stores before I started baking," Cora explains. "And although they had a lot of foods made from oat bran, when I checked a little closer, I found that few of them were truly cholesterol-free. And if they were, they tasted like cardboard. So I made my own. When they turned out so well and both Joe and my neighbor raved about them, I decided to go to the local grocery store and see if they would buy some from me. Of course, I had to check out the legalities first, but eventually I ended up with a contract to sell dozens of muffins and pies and cakes each week. To tell you the truth, I couldn't keep up with the orders. Plus I couldn't do the actual baking in my home due to health code regulations. So Joe and I rented a place and hired someone to do the baking, while Joe and I handled all the marketing from home. It was great! We made enough so that Joe could retire, and now we work together at home and neither of us has to leave the house. With one teenager still at home, I like that. I don't think children ever outgrow the need for someone to come home to. And with only a high school education and little or no job training, I certainly could never have made this much money working outside my home."

Sally's case was similar, although she and her husband, Mel, were much younger than Cora and Joe. When Mel was injured on the job, he was forced into early retirement. The disability settlement and their small savings were all they had to support themselves and their two preschoolers. Sally felt pressured to get a job, but she wondered who would care for her children, as well as Mel, who still needed occasional care and assistance. Besides, the only job experience Sally had was slinging hash during her college years before she and Mel married. How could she ever get a job that would bring in enough to cover all their expenses? Most of all, Sally didn't want to go off to work and leave her children and Mel in someone else's care. The decision was agonizing.

But even as Sally agonized, she prayed. And as she prayed, she sewed. Sewing had always been one of her greatest loves, and also one of her greatest talents. Sally made her own clothes, as well as her husband's shirts and many of her children's clothes. For Christmas and birthdays, all of her friends and family always got some special-made gift with Sally's initials stitched delicately in an unobtrusive spot.

One afternoon as Sally prayed and sewed the finishing touches on a blouse for her mother, she suddenly burst out laughing. Why hadn't she seen it before? She decided she had just been too close to the problem—as well as the solution—to see clearly. But now she was sure she had discovered God's answer to her prayers, because she realized beyond a shadow of a doubt what she was to do. She had no idea what her first step would be, but she knew she was going to start designing and manufacturing her own clothing line.

And that's exactly what she did. It took her a little while to work through all the legal ramifications, but once she did, she was off and selling!

"I've made more in the last three years working right here from my own home than I could ever have made working somewhere else. And I've loved every minute of it!"

Of course, not everyone wants or needs to take on such a mammoth project as supporting their entire family by baking cholesterol-free pastries or designing a whole new line of clothing, but even if you're just looking for a little extra money now and then, especially at Christmas or holiday time, there are many creative ways to use your talents to do just that—right from your own home.

Beth took up tole painting as a creative outlet after her first child was born and she had quit her job to stay home and be a full-time mommy. Financially, she didn't need to work so long as she and her husband stuck to their budget, and she loved staying home with her little daughter, but she felt a need for a hobby of some sort. Tole painting fit the bill.

In fact, she became so good at it that visitors to her home began to comment on her work and ask if she had ever considered selling any of it. Flattered, she admitted that it had never crossed her mind to do so, but she agreed to consider the possibility.

As the next holiday season approached, Beth saw an advertisement for available spaces in an upcoming pre-Christmas craft boutique. She decided to take the plunge. Renting a space at the boutique, she sold out of her entire stock of merchandise the first day. Needless to say, she started working on the following year's items immediately.

"It was so exciting," says Beth. "Not only did it give me a great sense of accomplishment to know that people would actually pay money for my creations, but I didn't have to cut into our tight budget to buy Christmas presents for friends and family. It's been the perfect answer for that little bit of extra income we needed."

But maybe you're already out working somewhere and you can't imagine giving up your job to come home and start a business of your own, especially if you can't think of anything particularly creative that you feel gifted to do. Well, that's the position I was in a few years ago. I was working as a part-time editor for a publishing house, and although I enjoyed the work, I really wanted to be home more.

I had heard about people who worked as writers and/or editors from their own homes, but I had no idea how to go about getting started in that field. So one day I took a deep breath, approached my boss at the publishing house, and told him what I'd been thinking.

To my great surprise—and joy—he wholeheartedly agreed with me that it was a wonderful idea, and he would be happy to have me start working for the company from my home. In fact, he told me he thought working at home was the "wave of the future." (According to the Small Business Administration's estimate, he was right. More than two million people now work full-time from their homes, with two-thirds of that number being women. Some New York marketing firms put that number at closer to six million, with a projected increase of 30 percent by the year 2000.) Within a few months I was happily completing assignments on my personal computer in my office at home. I have been here ever since.

Staying on at your current job but transferring it to your home, as I did, is a definite option. If your company doesn't have an existing work-at-home program, talk to them. You might be surprised at how eager they are to cooperate with you in setting up just such a program.

Whatever method(s) you use to make the adjustment from going out into the workplace every day to staying home with your family, remember to honor your Father God with the mother-heart by being faithful in your tithes and offerings, and then trusting Him to bring to pass the truth of Philippians 4:19 in your situation.

If you are faithful to seek His will for your life, God will make a way where there seems to be no way, and He will "supply all your need according to His riches in glory by Christ Jesus."

Childcare Alternatives for the Must-Work Mom

Despite the fact that statistics show more and more women becoming dissatisfied with outside employment and wanting to come home, and despite the fact that we have discussed several viable alternatives to working outside the home, and despite the fact that God's Word calls mothers home to raise and care for their childen, I know there are still mothers out there who sincerely believe they have no choice but to go out to work. For those of you who find yourselves in that position, this chapter is for you.

Whatever the reason may be that you find yourself going out into (or continuing in) the work force, one of your most difficult decisions is what to do with your children while you're gone. Every mother agonizes over this. Whether you're a stay-at-home mom or a mom with a job outside the home, your children's well-being is right up there at the top of your priority list. Because of that fact, it is vital for you to examine all the childcare options available before making a decision.

In *A Mother's Choice*, authors Paul Meier and Linda Burnett explain, "All of us must face the main problem with day care: that the care of the children is mainly impersonal custodial care because many women work with many different children. Therefore, the best substitute for your child in your absence would be *one* woman who keeps children in her home."[1] I certainly agree with that point because one familiar, long-term caretaker is certainly more reassuring to a child than several caretakers who may change shifts throughout the week. However, my personal choice for best caretaking arrangements (next to Mom herself, of course) is someone—particularly another family member—who will come into your home and care for your child.

The advantages to this situation are many. Not only will your child become familiar with and develop an ongoing relationship and attachment to the individual who comes into your home to care for him, but you won't be forced to drag your child out of bed in the early morning hours, taking him out into all sorts of weather and then displacing him by leaving him in unfamiliar surroundings. In addition, your child is less likely to be exposed to the many communicable diseases that run rampant among young children.

If and when your child should become ill, you probably won't be forced to make alternate childcare arrangements, since most individuals who come to your home will continue to do so even if your child has a cold or some other childhood illness. Most daycares, however, if they are aware of your child's condition, will ask you not to bring him when he isn't feeling well.

Unfortunately, family members or even close friends or neighbors who will come to your home to babysit on a daily basis are few and far between. Therefore, assuming you cannot find a dependable person to come to your home, I agree with the authors of *A Mother's Choice* that the next best alternative is to find a responsible, loving individual who will watch your child in her home. Although you will still have to contend with taking your child out every morning (and, if the caretaker keeps other children in her home, possibly exposing him to certain illnesses), there will still be one consistent figure for your child to relate to and grow to trust.

This situation, as any childcare situation, is not without potential problems. If the individual who cares for your child, whether she does so at your home or at hers, should become ill, you will have to find an acceptable substitute, sometimes at the last minute. If you are unable to do so, you may have to stay home from work until your babysitter recovers or until you make new childcare arrangements.

Another possible problem with a one-person caretaker for your child is that you as a mother may feel cheated and replaced by the caretaker. It is not unusual for an infant or very young child to become emotionally attached to the person who cares for him during most of his waking hours. My friend Darlene once told me how crushed she felt when she went to the babysitter's home to pick up her 18-month-old daughter, Shana. When she reached out to take her toddler from the sitter's arms, Shana refused to come to her, clinging instead to the woman who had cared for her throughout the day. Other mothers have told me of their heartbreak upon arriving at the babysitter's home, only to find out that their child took his first step or spoke his first word while they were at work—experiences that no parent wants to miss.

A primary concern for all mothers, whether leaving their children with an individual caretaker or at an institutional daycare facility, is the quality of care provided. Individual caretakers, as well as daycare facilities, must be licensed. This license limits the number of children an individual caretaker may oversee as well as the number of children allowable in a daycare facility, based on the number of workers on hand. It is vital that you ensure that these limitations are being enforced, wherever you choose to leave your child while you are gone to work.

But even if your childcare facility complies with the license requirements for number of children per worker, you may feel that the number is too high to ensure proper care for your child. An easy rule of thumb to gauge whether your child will receive adequate care is to go by your child's age. In other words, if a child is one year old or less, there should be a ratio of one worker per child. If the child is two years old, the ratio could drop to one worker for every two children, then one worker for every three children if they are three years old, and so on. That ratio may sound a bit stringent, but the younger the child, the more individual and constant care is required. For your child's sake, don't settle for less.

Marianne did. She had been looking for a job for months to help supplement their already meager family income, which had shrunk even more when her husband was laid off and had to take a lower-paying job. Although she had checked in the yellow pages for nearby childcare facilities, she really hadn't spent any time touring them or talking to other parents who left their children there. Consequently, when a company to which she had applied for a job called her and asked her to come to work immediately, she felt she had no time to do much research on the different childcare options in her neighborhood. Instead, she enrolled her nine-month-old son, Joey, in the first one that offered her an opening.

The next morning was one of the most difficult of her life. Not only did she have to get up early to get herself ready to start a new job, but she had to wake her son, dress and feed him, and then take him to the daycare where she was to leave him for slightly over nine hours. Her heart was breaking as she handed him over to the daycare director, who tried in vain to silence Joey's cries. Marianne's last image of her son, as she forced herself to walk out the door, was of him screaming hysterically, reaching out his chubby arms toward her as tears flowed from his frightened blue eyes.

"Joey will be fine," she told herself time and time again throughout her first day on the job. "He'll get used to it. And it's a good facility. They assured me that they meet all the necessary requirements. I have nothing to worry about. He'll be just fine."

But he wasn't just fine. At 5:30 P.M., when Marianne arrived to pick up Joey, he was sitting in a crib over in the corner of the room. His diaper and the crib sheet were urine-soaked, and Joey was still crying.

When Marianne asked the harried worker why Joey hadn't been changed, she replied that there just hadn't been time. There were too many other children to attend to, she explained.

What Marianne learned that day was, although the daycare met state requirements for the worker-to-child ratio, there was still too much work and too many children for the workers to take care of properly.

"I went home in tears," Marianne recalls. "I didn't know what to do. Here I had just started a new job, so I certainly couldn't ask for any time off to make appropriate childcare arrangements. And I knew I could never take Joey back to that daycare. So I did the only thing I could think of to do—I quit! Then, after taking the time to line up a responsible sitter to come into my home, I went job-hunting once again. Although it took me quite awhile to find something, I never regretted my decision to pull Joey out of that overcrowded facility. I could never have lived with myself if I had taken him back there day after day simply so I could hang on to my job. No job is worth that."

No job indeed. No matter how many jobs you must pass up or how many hours you must spend searching for the right childcare situation, it is imperative that your child's well-being be your first priority when considering going out to work. We have all heard the horror stories of the daycares that appeared to be well-run, safe, and secure facilities, yet turned out to be nothing more than high-priced "kiddie parking lots"—or worse.

Is there a way to avoid placing your child in that sort of situation? Is there a foolproof way of selecting your child's daycare arrangements? Well, I believe I would be remiss both as a mother and as a Christian if I suggested starting your childcare search anywhere but on your knees—and hopefully the first thing you will ask the Lord is whether or not you are even to consider going out to work! If there is an alternative to doing so, He's the One who knows what that alternative is. And I am confident that He will enable you to discover that alternative, since He is the heavenly Father with the mother-heart, who longs to see earthly mothers at home caring for their children.

But if, after seeking God's will concerning your working outside the home, you still feel that you are to go out and find a job, begin immediately to seek His guidance as to the proper situation in which to place your child while you are gone. One possibility is a church-run daycare. Perhaps your own church has such a facility, which would be a real plus, since you probably know many of the workers involved. Besides that, church-run daycares often offer a discount to church members. But if your church does not offer such a service, don't automatically assume that any facility that is sponsored by a church is appropriate. Check them out as closely and carefully as you would any nonchurch facility. And no matter who runs the daycare, whether it's a church or not, if you aren't personally acquainted with the facility's workers and/or its policies, ask the prospective facility for names of longtime clients. Other parents will certainly understand your concern for your child's welfare, and will be happy to discuss what they have learned about the facility during the time their children have been there.

Also, insist on the right to drop in unannounced and visit the facility at any time during the day. A reputable daycare will have no objections to such a reasonable request; in fact, they will probably welcome and encourage your concern for your child's well-being.

A couple of additional things to keep in mind about daycares is that many will not take a child under a certain age, particularly if they are not potty-trained. If you are considering returning to the work force while you still have an infant at home, you may have to look a lot harder to find a facility that will accommodate your needs. Also, if you have more than one child, ask about family rates. Many facilities give a discount for the second or third child in a family. And, although they are scarce and often have a waiting list, there are daycares who charge on a sliding scale, according to your income.

Another option that has worked for some mothers, particularly those who work part-time, is a babysitting co-op. A co-op can be a group of mothers who trade off babysitting on a regular or as-needed basis; it can also be a state-run or private facility that requires occasional parental participation in exchange for lowered rates. This arrangement may work particularly well for those moms who work only a few hours each week, or who do not have an outside job but feel the need for an occasional break from their little ones. Also, being actively involved as an occasional worker reassures you of the type of care and programs being provided for your child.

One alternative that my son Mike and his wife, Christy, tried—albeit unsuccessfuly—was alternating their work schedules so that one of them would always be home with their young son, Mikey. The problem with that was, Christy was working all night and then trying to sleep during the day when Mikey wanted to play. It didn't take them long to decide that this system was not for them. However, I have known of couples who claim it worked for their families.

According to *Jobs '92*, by Kathryn and Ross Petras, another childcare option is the growing trend within the business world for companies to offer on-site childcare facilities or other childcare options for their employees. In fact, the authors refer to experts who "predict that by the end of the decade, about half of all people in the work force will be responsible for children, elderly parents, or both. One of the best solutions: employer-provided intergenerational daycare, daycare for both children and elderly parents."[2]

These companies are referred to as "family-friendly"

because they offer not only on-site daycare but job flexibility as well. Examples of job flexibility include part-time schedules, flextime, job sharing, and at-home work (a definitely viable option which we discussed in a previous chapter). All of these options are points to consider and discuss with prospective or existing employers.

One very important issue I don't want to ignore at this point is that of mothers who manage to stay home while they have preschoolers, yet feel the need to return to the work force once their children are in school for several hours each day. I wholeheartedly support this concept of staying home at least until your children are in school, but feel the need to emphasize the fact that just because children are in school until 2:00 or 3:00 P.M. each afternoon does not mean they are old enough to care for themselves for those few hours between the time they get out of school and Mom gets home from work.

There are entirely too many latchkey children in our society today—as our rising juvenile crime rate can attest. My youngest child is now a teenager in high school, and yet I always try to be here to greet him when he gets home in the afternoon. Although he may not stay longer than the few minutes it takes to drop off his books and grab something out of the refrigerator to eat, it gives him a sense of security to know that I'm here if he's had a rough day and just needs someone to talk to. And, let's face it, my being here prevents our home from being used as a free-for-all hangout for unsupervised teens to get involved in immoral or even illegal behavior. Oh, I know, once kids hit a certain age, if they want to get into trouble, they'll find a place to do it. But why allow your home to be that place?

So if you have come to that time in your life when you feel you can feasibly go out to work now that your children are all in school during the day, consider seriously what they will do in their afternoon hours—not to mention during school vacations. The best choice, of course, is for you to find a part-time job where you can make it home before the kids do. However, unless you can find a job where you will have school vacations off with your kids—and there aren't many of those jobs around—you will still need to consider some of the childcare options we've already discussed: someone to come into your home, a friend or neighbor who will watch your child at her home, a daycare facility, or even an after-school program right on the grounds of your child's school. Any of those choices are preferable to sending him home to an empty house to sit in front of the television set until you get home.

Whatever your child's age and whatever your financial and childcare needs, before blindly accepting that full-time position and placing your child in an all-day childcare facility five days a week, prayerfully consider your choices and their possible ramifications.

And then remember the story of Nathan.

I met Nathan on the first day of my job at a daycare center where I worked some years ago. Nathan was an adorable little three-year-old with curly blond hair and the saddest big blue eyes you ever saw. He didn't talk much, but he took every opportunity to crawl up on my lap and snuggle close while he sucked his thumb. Sometimes I read to him or sang him a few songs, but it didn't really seem to matter to him one way or the other. He just wanted me to hold him close.

Except on Fridays. Nathan came to life every Friday afternoon right after naptime. His eyes would begin to sparkle with excitement and anticipation as he would run back and forth from the window, where he would peer out anxiously toward the parking lot and ask me, "What time is it, Teacher? How much longer till 5:30?"

Five-thirty, you see, was the time his mother arrived to pick him up. Even though Nathan was barely three years old, he had already learned the meaning of that old saying, "T.G.I.F."—"Thank God it's Friday!" As he so eloquently put it, Friday afternoon at 5:30 meant, "Now I gots two whole days to play with my mommy!"

I only pray that Nathan's mommy was able to spend as much of her weekends as possible playing with that curly-haired little boy who waited so patiently for her for five long days every week. Somehow I doubted her job was worth the wait.

Motherhood: A Season for Joy

For 26 years I believed there was no stronger love than that of a mother and child. Undoubtedly that had a lot to do with the fact that I was separated from my children for a time after my divorce in 1969. I missed them so much, and I can remember thinking that I would do absolutely anything to have them back.

Then, on July 5, 1974, I found out that God had felt exactly the same way about me. He loved me and yearned for me—so much so that He sent His Son to die for my sin and to provide the way for me to return to Him.

It was at this point that I understood there was an even greater love than that of an earthly mother for her child, and that it was the love of the heavenly Father for His children.

Most of us are familiar with the saying, "God couldn't be everywhere, so He made mothers." That may not be too theologically sound, since we know that the omnipresent God is indeed everywhere, but it certainly emphasizes the truth that God designed motherhood to be the expression of His mother-heart here on earth. What a privilege to have the opportunity of reflecting God's love to others—particularly our children!

And yet we allow ourselves to get so caught up in the pursuit of "things" that we lose sight of the importance of what motherhood is all about. Our priorities become rear-ranged, and before we know it the lion's share of our time and energy becomes centered on this temporal life here on earth rather than on those things which will last for eter-nity. We become more focused on the concern that our children have nice clothes, live in a good neighborhood, go to the best schools, take piano lessons, and play on the soccer team than whether or not they come to know Jesus as Lord and Savior. This is not the mother-heart of God in action; this is selling out to the world system.

Now don't get me wrong—there is nothing inherently wrong with nice clothes or good schools or piano lessons. To want those things for ourselves and our children is also not wrong. But it is time for us to refocus our attention on those things that are truly important, those things that will not pass away when this life is over.

One of the best ways to do this is to reflect on the wise words of King Solomon in Ecclesiastes 3, where he reminds us, "To everything there is a season, a time for every pur-pose under heaven" (verse 1). There are times, especially as busy, exhausted, harried mothers of several active pre-schoolers, when women feel as if they'll never again have a moment to themselves. They begin to believe that life as they once knew it is over for them, that they have been reduced to mindless robots who change diapers and make peanut-butter-and-jelly sandwiches on command. Their daily conversations are limited to short sentences of one-syllable words: "Get down from there right now!"; "Put that down or else!"; "Leave her alone!" and "For the last time, stop that!"

And yet all too soon those little rug-rats and curtain-climbers are going to their senior proms and high school graduations, then leaving for college or getting married and having children of their own. And we are left behind to listen to the deafening silence and wonder how it all could have passed so quickly.

Seasons. A time for every purpose under heaven. That's what it's all about. For a season we are mothers of little ones who demand and require the bulk of our time and attention. But there are other seasons as well—seasons when we are free to explore and develop and create, seasons when we will serve God just as surely as when we were raising our little ones, but perhaps in a different area of ministry.

In *The Curious Waltz of the Working Woman*, authors Karen Scalf Linamen and Linda Holland have adapted King Solomon's pronouncements of wisdom in Ecclesiastes 3 to speak right to the heart of today's woman who may be feeling pressured to yield to the world's demands and expectations rather than standing firm in what God has called her to do and be today.

> There is an appointed time for everything.
> And there is a time for every event under heaven—
> A time to plant, and a time to reap.
> A time to strive, and a time to rest.
> A time to cook, and a time to create jobs for the fast-food industry.
> A time to clean the house, and a time to shrug and pull the shades.
> A time to help, and a time to be helped.
> A time to give, and a time to take.
> A time to seek the praises of a boss,
>   and a time to cultivate the love of a child.
> A time to strive to meet a deadline,
>   and a time to strive to build a family.
> A time to go to work, and a time to turn your heart toward home.
> A time to confront, and a time to give in.
> A time to network with your peers,
>   and a time to rekindle the fires of a marriage.
> A time to earn, and a time to spend.
> A time to accumulate, and a time to give away.

A time to minister to friends,
and a time to evaluate the state of your own heart.
A time to say yes, and a time to say no.
A time for material wealth,
and a time to pursue the greater riches of the soul.[1]

None of us likes change. Change is hard, and we prefer easy to hard. But if we are going to grow and mature as women and as Christians, change is inevitable. We think we want children, but when we have them our life is forever changed. In fact, someone once said that deciding to have children is like deciding to let your heart walk around outside your body for the rest of your life. And it's true. Once you have held your very first child in your arms, once you have gazed into those trusting eyes and nuzzled the warm softness of your baby's cheek, you will never be the same. You have entered a new season of life, and you truly begin to understand that you are no longer "your own" (see 1 Corinthians 6:19).

But that season will not last forever, although it may seem like it at the time. Eventually you will find yourself without those little ones under your feet. In fact, even those trying teenage years will pass. (I promise!) And you will find yourself, once again, in a new season of life—a season of just as much opportunity and promise as the last, yet different, as each season must be.

And don't think that this transition will be easier than the last. With all the trials and pressures that come with being a mother, it is often difficult to let go of that season of life known as motherhood and move on to the next. Sociologists and others have termed it the "empty-nest" syndrome; feminists have warned that, without a career, empty-nest syndrome is inevitable for those who choose to be "just a wife and mother."

But it need not be so. When we learn to view our lives in progressive seasons, living each season fully, as God intended, we will not feel cheated when it is time to make the transition to the next season of life. True, a woman who has found her sole identity in being a mother will undoubtedly suffer from depression and loss of identity when her grown children move on to start lives of their own. But the same is true of women (and men) who base their identity on their jobs or careers. We have all known people who eagerly looked forward to their retirement years, only to discover that when the time finally arrived they seemed to lose their zeal for living, wasting away in self-pity and memories of "the good old days."

The reason for this is that these people have never understood that their true identity is found only in Jesus Christ. When our first priority is love and service to Him, the other priorities—including and especially mother-hood—will all fall into line. That's why Jesus said, when asked which was the greatest commandment of all, " 'You shall love the Lord your God with all your heart, with all your soul, and with all your mind.' This is the first and great commandment. And the second is like it: 'You shall love your neighbor as yourself.' On these two commandments hang all the Law and the Prophets" (Matthew 22:37-40).

What Jesus has proclaimed here is the answer to the question that is in everyone's heart, whether Christian or non-Christian: "How then shall we live?" It is the question that each of us begins asking from the moment of conception. And because we are all born in sin (see Psalm 51:5), we decide early on that the answer to that question is to live for self.

Watch any baby and you will see that truth in action. If the infant is tired or hungry or wet, it makes absolutely no difference that his parents are exhausted from already getting up with him five times that night. He is going to cry and scream until his needs are met. Each of us grows up believing that the universe revolves around us, and we live accordingly. Most of us have learned to modify our behavior in order to live within the dictates of society, but other people never seem to learn this, and both they and society reap the results.

But it is only as we come face-to-face with a holy and just God that, regardless of our outward behavior, we finally see ourselves for the totally corrupt, self-centered, sinful creatures that we really are. As the prophet Isaiah said when he beheld the glory of the Lord, "Woe is me, for I am undone! Because I am a man of unclean lips, and I dwell in the midst of a people of unclean lips; for my eyes have seen the King, the Lord of hosts" (Isaiah 6:5).

Once our eyes have seen the King, the Lord of hosts, we know, like Isaiah, that it is impossible to try to justify ourselves any longer. We realize that there is absolutely nothing we can do to earn our way into God's holiness. But even as we come face-to-face with the holy and just God, we also come heart-to-heart with His mercy and grace and unconditional love—the love that says, "Yes, you're right. You are a sinful creature with no right to come into my presence. You deserve nothing more than death and hell. But I love you anyway—so much so that I sent my Son to die in your place. Death and hell no longer hold any power over you, if you accept my Son's sacrifice and acknowledge Him as Lord and Savior of your life. Then, in His name, you may come boldly and freely into my presence, because you will be my child and I will be your Father, and I will change you to become all I created you to be. I will also be your mother, and I will teach you to be the mother I have called you to be. But it must all be done in my way and in my time."

Seasons. God's seasons, not ours. Seasons in which to grow and flourish and blossom and reproduce—and change. Although God encourages us to look forward to the next season with anticipation, He does not want us to run ahead of Him and try to live in the next season before the present season has been fulfilled. That's why He calls us to obedience *today*. He knows that one day at a time is all we can handle. As Jesus said, "Therefore do not worry about tomorrow, for tomorrow will worry about its own things. Sufficient for the day is its own trouble" (Matthew 6:34).

Deuteronomy 8:1 puts it a different way: "Every commandment which I command you *today* you must be careful to observe, that you may live and multiply, and go in and possess the land of which the Lord swore to your fathers" (italics mine). God's Word is full of a lot of promises about possessing the land, but each of those promises is contingent on walking in obedience to His Word *today*. Not tomorrow, for tomorrow will take care of itself. And certainly not yesterday, for yesterday is gone, and we cannot relive it. If we failed to walk as He called us to walk yesterday, it will do us no good to beat ourselves for that failure. Instead, we must ask for and receive God's forgiveness (see 1 John 1:9), and then go on and seek His grace to walk according to His Word *today*. When we do that, Deuteronomy 8:1 promises that we will live and multiply and go in and possess the land that He has promised to us. Worrying about tomorrow or dwelling on yesterday will rob us of all that God has promised us for *today*.

And if today you find yourself in the position of mother, rejoice! For remember that God has ordained that motherhood be joyful (see Psalm 113:9). And because you are the model here on earth of His great mother-heart, then know also that God has ordained that motherhood be an honorable position. You are not "*just* a wife and/or mother"; you are participating in the most honorable profession any woman can ever fulfill. You are partnering with the Creator in raising a godly generation to His glory.

The world may tell you otherwise, implying that you are not being "all you can be." But they do not understand that you are fulfilling God's purposes for your life in this season. You are walking in obedience to His will for your life today, and that is all He holds You accountable for.

It has been said that, at the end of life, no one ever says, "Gee, I wish I had spent more time at the office." In *The Best Jobs in America for Parents*, by Susan Bacon Dynerman and

Lynn O'Rourke Hayes, the authors found countless surveys and studies to substantiate that sentiment:

- According to a 1986 *Fortune* survey of two-income families with children under 12, not only 26 percent of women but also 30 percent of men turned down promotions, transfers, or new jobs for the plain and simple reason that it would have cut back on their time with their families;

- In 1989, a poll by the *Washington Post* and ABC News found that 56 percent of working mothers as well as 43 percent of working fathers had reduced their working hours to spend more time with their children;

- Robert Half International discovered that almost 80 percent of the men and women in this country would sacrifice career opportunities for more family time.

According to the authors, "The message is simple. *I need more time. Time at home. Time for me. But, more than anything else, time with my children.*"[2]

Because children grow up. Quickly. Before you know it, this season will be over, and if it has been spent doing anything other than what God has commanded daily, the next season will bring no more fulfillment than the last. Living life apart from God's will is empty and meaningless. King Solomon, who was noted not only for his great wisdom but also for his vast wealth, discovered that everything he had done or accumulated in his lifetime apart from God "was vanity and grasping for the wind. There was no profit under the sun" (Ecclesiastes 2:11). But he also learned that God "has made everything beautiful *in its time*" (Ecclesiastes 3:11, italics mine). When we, like the apostle Paul, "have learned in whatever state I am, to be content" (Philippians 4:11), we will find that "everything [is] beautiful in its time."

Whether we are just beginning to make the transition into the season of motherhood or moving toward the end of that season and into the next, life can be beautiful and fulfilling if we are seeking to walk in daily obedience to God's call on our lives. Don't let the world's distortions of success move you off that path of daily obedience and rob you of even one day of the joy that God has planned for you as a partner with Him in motherhood.

And remember: God is faithful even when we're not. If for any reason you have been separated from your children (as I was for a time), know that God is a God of restoration. Where we have failed, He brings success. When we fall, He picks us up. When we sin, He forgives. He never leaves us or forsakes us. His love, because He is our heavenly Father and also has a mother-heart, is so much greater for us than our love is for our children. Therefore we can trust Him to lead us into the right decisions and solutions to the "Should-I-go-out-to-work-or-should-I-stay-home-with-my-kids" dilemma.

Most of all, the next time our kids call out, "Mommy, where are you?" we can trust Him to give us the right answer.

Notes

Chapter 2—Good Mommies/Bad Mommies

1. Karen Scalf Linamen and Linda Holland, *The Curious Waltz of the Working Woman* (Ventura, CA: Regal Books, 1990).
2. Betty Friedan, *The Feminine Mystique* (New York: Dell Publishing, 1984).

Chapter 3—I Want My Mommy!

1. Sister Mary Rose McGeady, *God's Lost Children* (Hollywood, CA: Covenant House California, 1991).
2. Brenda Hunter, Ph.D., *Home by Choice* (Portland: Multnomah Press, 1991).

Chapter 4—What About Mr. Mom?

1. Sylvia Porter, "Housewives Contribute Billions to Economy" (*Los Angeles Times* syndicate).

Chapter 5—Don't Bother Mommy, She's Busy

1. H. Norman Wright, *Always Daddy's Girl* (Ventura, CA: Regal Books, 1989).
2. Heather Harpham, *Daddy, Where Were You?* (Lynnwood, WA: Aglow Publications, 1991).
3. Hunter, *Choice*.

Chapter 6—The Sandwich Mommy

1. Ruth Bathauer, *Parent Care* (Ventura, CA: Regal Books, 1990).
2. Eugenia Anderson-Ellis and Marsha Dryan, *Aging Parents and You* (New York: Master Media Limited, 1988), p. 10.

Chapter 9—Childcare Alternatives for the Must-Work Mom

1. Paul Meier and Linda Burnett, *A Mother's Choice* (Grand Rapids: Baker Book House, 1980).
2. Kathryn and Ross Petras, *Jobs '92* (New York: Prentice Hall Press, 1992).

Chapter 10: Motherhood: A Season for Joy

1. Karen Scalf Linamen and Linda Holland, *The Curious Waltz of the Working Woman* (Ventura, CA: Regal Books, 1990). Used by permission.
2. Susan Bacon Dynerman and Lynn O'Rourke Hayes, *The Best Jobs in America for Parents* (New York: Ballantine Books, 1991).

Other Good Harvest House Reading

GETTING THE BEST OUT OF YOUR KIDS
by *Kevin Leman*

Time-tested advice and a healthy dose of humor are nationally recognized psychologist Keven Leman's prescription for great parenting. Dr. Leman offers solutions to the toughest problems parents face and gives practical advice on raising kids from start to finish. This information-rich book also includes a special section on the character traits of oldest, middle, and youngest children and how to adjust your parenting to fit.

TOO HURRIED TO LOVE
by *Charles Bradshaw* and *Dave Gilbert*

You know the feeling.... Your spouse is in shock when you remember a birthday. The kids can't believe it when you make it to their games. And it's been so long since you had coffee with friends that you've forgotten who your friends are! You're busy, but are you busy doing what matters? If it's time for midcourse corrections, this book will help. *Too Hurried to Love* is a "roadmap in a book" that will guide you to living with simplicity and purpose.

MORE TO LIFE THAN HAVING IT ALL
by *Bob Welch*

Full-time careers, full-time families, full-time hobbies... By the end of the day, it can feel like a moral victory just to have a measurable pulse! In his relaxed, enjoyable style, award-winning journalist Bob Welch offers valuable insight on how we can shed cultural values for eternal ones. His poignant, often humorous illustrations will not only make you laugh and cry but will also cause you to evaluate your priorities.

QUIET TIMES FOR COUPLES
by *H. Norman Wright*

Noted counselor and author Norm Wright provides the help you need to nurture your oneness in Christ. In a few moments together each day you will discover a deeper, richer intimacy with each other and with God, sharing your fondest dreams and deepest thoughts— creating memories of quiet times together.

THE STAY-AT-HOME MOM
by *Donna Otto*

Applauding the stay-at-home mom, author Donna Otto takes on the challenges and highlights the rewards of staying at home. With boundless enthusiasm for home and personal organization, Otto cheers on the stay-at-home mom and provides practical ideas to make the journey an adventure. This book will help you know whether being a stay-at-home mom is right for *you*.